Disasters of War

Callot Goya Dix

Disasters of War
Callot Goya Dix

National Touring Exhibitions

Published on the occasion of Disasters of War: Callot, Goya, Dix, a National Touring Exhibition organised by the Hayward Gallery, London for the Arts Council of England in collaboration with the Department of Prints and Drawings, British Museum

Exhibition tour

Art Gallery and Museum, Kelvingrove, Glasgow	7 March - 19 April 1998
Oriel Mostyn, Llandudno	25 April - 30 May
Whitworth Art Gallery, Manchester	20 June - 16 August
Brighton Museum and Art Gallery	22 August - 4 October
Durham Art Gallery	17 October - 15 November
Wolverhampton Art Gallery and Museum	23 January - 20 March 1999

Exhibition organised by Roger Malbert, assisted by Jessica White

Catalogue designed by Alexander Boxill
Printed by Amica Fine Art Print Limited, UK

Cover: Otto Dix, *Field of shell craters near Dontrien lit up by flares,* 1924 (detail)
(plate 4) © DACS 1998

ISBN 1 85332 169 9

National Touring Exhibitions, Hayward Gallery and Arts Council Collection publications are distributed by Cornerhouse Publications, 70 Oxford Street, Manchester M1 5NH (telephone 0161 237 9662; facsimile 0161 237 9664).

Preface

Disasters of War consists of works from three series of etchings - Jacques Callot's *Miseries of War,* Goya's *The Disasters of War* and Otto Dix's *War* - which are separated from each other by centuries. The first was published in Paris in 1633; the second was executed between 1810 and 1820, and published posthumously in Madrid in 1863; the last was issued in Berlin in 1924. Although stylistically and formally unalike, the series are links in a chain. They belong to one of the greatest traditions of European war art, that of realism and protest.

There is no need to stress the relevance of these works to the present. The imagery of war is all too familiar. The questions that arise today from the camera's view of war can be asked as well of these graphic depictions of human suffering and destruction: what relationship exists between horror and beauty, between sympathy and voyeurism, revulsion and curiosity? The three series record different wars, but each reminds us of the perennial misery that war unleashes: they show the plight of its victims.

Three authoritative essays by eminent historians give detailed accounts of the series and place them in their historical context. Antony Griffiths, who writes on Callot, is Keeper of Prints and Drawings at the British Museum and author of *Prints and Printmaking,* as well as various catalogues of exhibitions of prints held at the British Museum; Juliet Wilson-Bareau, who writes on Goya, is author of the standard catalogue of Goya's complete works and of *Goya's Prints,* as well as other exhibition catalogues in Britain and abroad; John Willett, who writes on Dix, is a translator and editor of the English edition of Bertold Brecht's writings, has written on the arts of

Weimar Germany and recently translated Brecht's *War Primer,* eighty epigrams to a selection of war photographs. Together the essays provide an indispensable introduction to these powerful, passionate works which remain as vivid today as when they were created.

All the prints come from the British Museum; the exhibition is the latest in the series, organised by the Hayward Gallery's National Touring Exhibitions in collaboration with the Museum's Department of Prints and Drawings, whose purpose is to make the wealth of that collection accessible to a wider public across the country.

Susan Ferleger Brades
Director, Hayward Gallery

Roger Malbert
Senior Curator, National Touring Exhibitions, Hayward Gallery

Contents

Callot

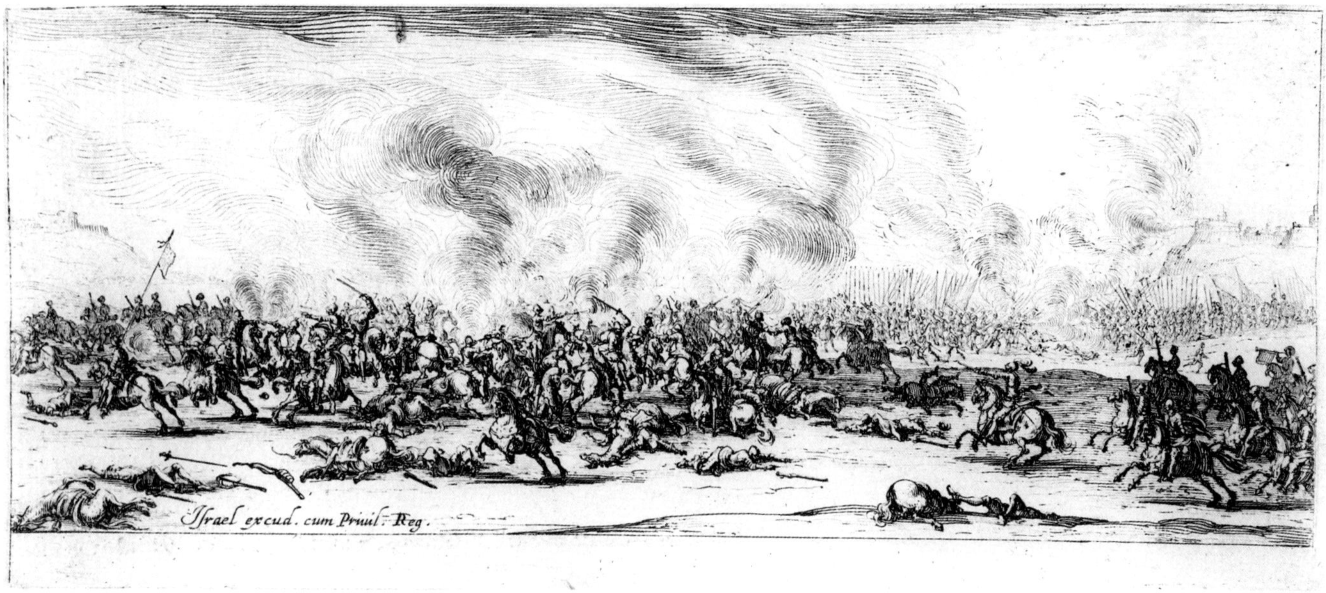

Miseries of War, 1633 (large format)

Plate 3
Battle scene

Callot: Miseries of War

Antony Griffiths

Jacques Callot's so-called *Large Miseries of War* was published in Paris by his friend Israel Henriet in 1633. It consists of a title page and seventeen oblong plates, all of the same small size and numbered consecutively from 1 to 18. It has long been regarded as his masterpiece and remains the best-known set of prints made in seventeenth-century France.

By the 1630s, the art of printmaking had been practised in western Europe for about two hundred years, and had grown from a sideline of a few goldsmiths into a very large international business. Thousands of plates were being produced every year across Europe, and the trade had already established clear conventions of type, format and subject-matter. Those who worked in it had begun to specialise, and designers, publishers and printers were in many cases quite distinct professions from the actual printmakers. These were themselves divided into engravers, etchers and woodcutters, depending on which of the various printmaking processes they used.

Within this large and crowded world, Callot was very soon recognised to be an original who was unlike any who had come before him and who stood apart from his contemporaries. He made plates in vast numbers - his output over twenty-five years was more than 1400. Most were less than two or three inches in width, but a few were assembled from large plates into wall-plans, five or six feet in size. Almost all of his prints he designed himself, and a good number of his preparatory drawings survive.

The technique he used was invariably etching, but he developed or adapted a special tool, known as the *échoppe*, which imitated the line produced by the engraver's burin. This enabled him to mimic the aesthetic effect of the swelling and narrowing line of the then very fashionable engraving, while maintaining the speed of production that can only be achieved with etching. His style was instantly recognisable, and his small balletic figures marked out his work from all his competitors. Soon collectors began to notice him and to form albums containing as many of his prints as they could lay their hands on. Already in 1688 La Bruyère included among his *Caractères* a man who was tormented by his inability to find the last print he needed to complete his collection of Callot's works.

Callot's achievement was all the more remarkable given the unpromising ambience in which he was brought up. He was born in 1592 in Nancy, the capital of Lorraine. This is a district now in eastern France, separated from the Rhine border with Germany by Alsace. But during Callot's life it was an independent Duchy whose historic affiliations were as much with Germany as France. It was French-speaking and was only a hundred and fifty miles east from Paris so connections with France were always close. Nancy was a backwater, a town rather than a city, and it was not large enough to give scope to any great talent. Callot's father was herald-at-arms to the Dukes of Lorraine and it was this that gave him the title to nobility that his son inherited. Jean Callot apprenticed his son to the court goldsmith, doubtless intending him to become his successor. But the young Jacques soon discovered a gift for drawing and at the age of sixteen or seventeen left for Italy. He had made one or two prints before his departure and in Rome he worked for Philippe Thomassin, a French engraver who had made a career for himself there. So it was in Rome that he learnt the craft of the printmaker and perfected his skills in the medium.

In 1614, he moved from Rome to Florence and set himself up as an independent artist, working mostly for the Dukes of Tuscany. This was the great age of Florentine masques and court entertainments and Callot's style was indelibly marked by his experience of recording these evanescent but magnificent affairs for posterity. It was these prints that began to spread his fame and brought him to the attention of the Duke of Lorraine, who wanted to attract such a famous native son back home. So with the promise of accommodation and considerable financial support Callot returned to Nancy in 1621, where he settled for the rest of his life. The Duke probably led him to expect that he would be given numerous commissions, but this, like most of his promises, was never fulfilled. So to earn his livelihood, and to maintain his wife whom he married in 1623, Callot was forced to produce a stream of prints that would produce the necessary income.

From this much followed. There had to be lots of prints. They had to be new and varied in subject and different in style. They had to be printed in large numbers and this pushed him into making them in sets. In this way, for the same amount of effort in marketing, one could get six, twelve or more times the income. He was helped by his friend, Israel Henriet, the son of the court painter in Nancy who had been in Italy at the same time in the 1610s. Henriet settled in Paris, the only French-speaking place where the market for prints was large enough for an artist to support himself by their sale, and acted as Callot's publisher, advancing him money against future plates and offering him hospitality when he came to Paris on business.

The set of the *Miseries of War* is the most famous product of this partnership. It was sold as a small booklet and the eighteen sheets were stitched together at the left side. The purchaser could either bind the sheets together between hard covers - adding other small plates if he wished - or trim off the margins and paste each into a blank collector's album. For really serious collectors, sets were printed before the lines of verses were added by a specialist writing engraver in the margins underneath the designs. In this way they had the assurance that they owned one of the first impressions taken off the plate when it was at its freshest, before the lines had begun to wear down with the action of repeated printing. The prints illustrated here are from one of the few surviving such sets, and the lack of margins shows that they were once in an album. The six lines of verse that were added later to each print are said to have been composed by one famous collector, the abbé de Marolles, whose enormous collection forms the foundation of the Cabinet des Estampes in the Bibliothèque Nationale in Paris.

The French title is *Les misères et malheurs de la guerre* , the 'miseries and misfortunes of war'. It was this title that Goya deliberately echoed in choosing as a title for his series *The Disasters of War*. Yet those who examine Callot's prints closely - and their small size and crowded detail require careful study - are soon puzzled to find that the title does not really correspond to what they see. The sequence begins with the recuitment of new soldiers and their bloodying in battle. Then things begin to fall apart. We next find the soldiers plundering farmhouses and torturing the inhabitants to get them to reveal where they have hidden their wealth. They move on to churches, convents and villages. By now all semblance of military discipline is lost. They have become mere highway robbers who are hunted out by the authorities in their lairs in the woods. Once they are captured they meet with ferocious punishment: they are dropped from the strappado, hung, shot, burnt and broken on the wheel. Some end up as cripples in hospitals or have to seek alms from the very peasants

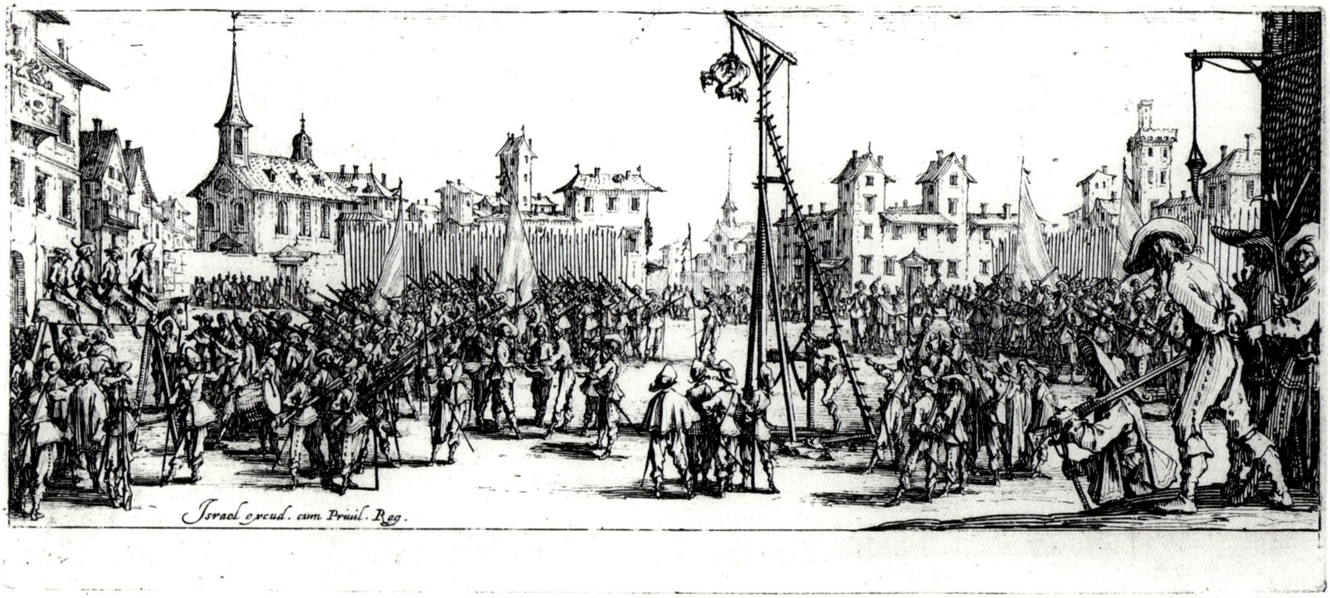

Plate 10
The strappado

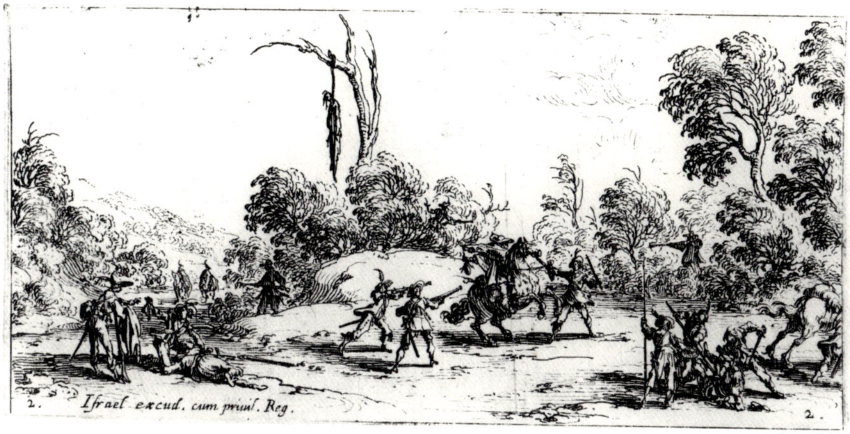

Miseries of War, 1636 (small format)

Plate 2
Attack on the highway

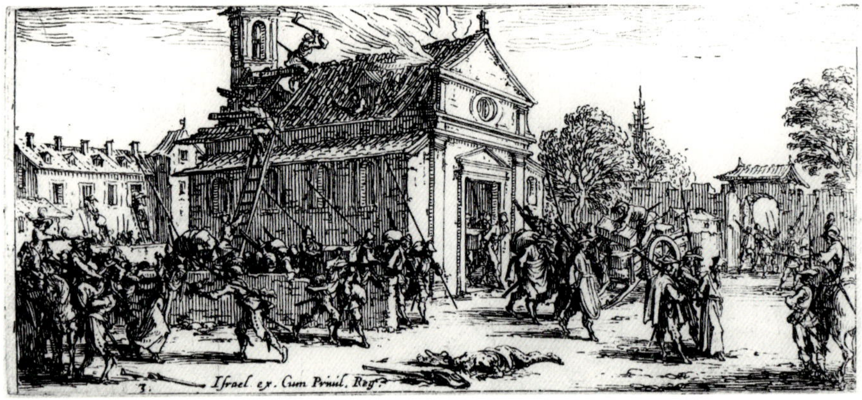

Plate 3

Destruction of a convent

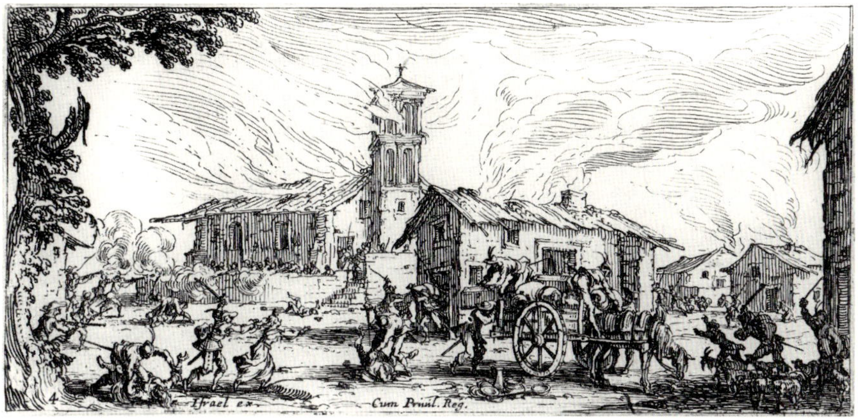

Plate 4

Plundering and burning a village

Goya

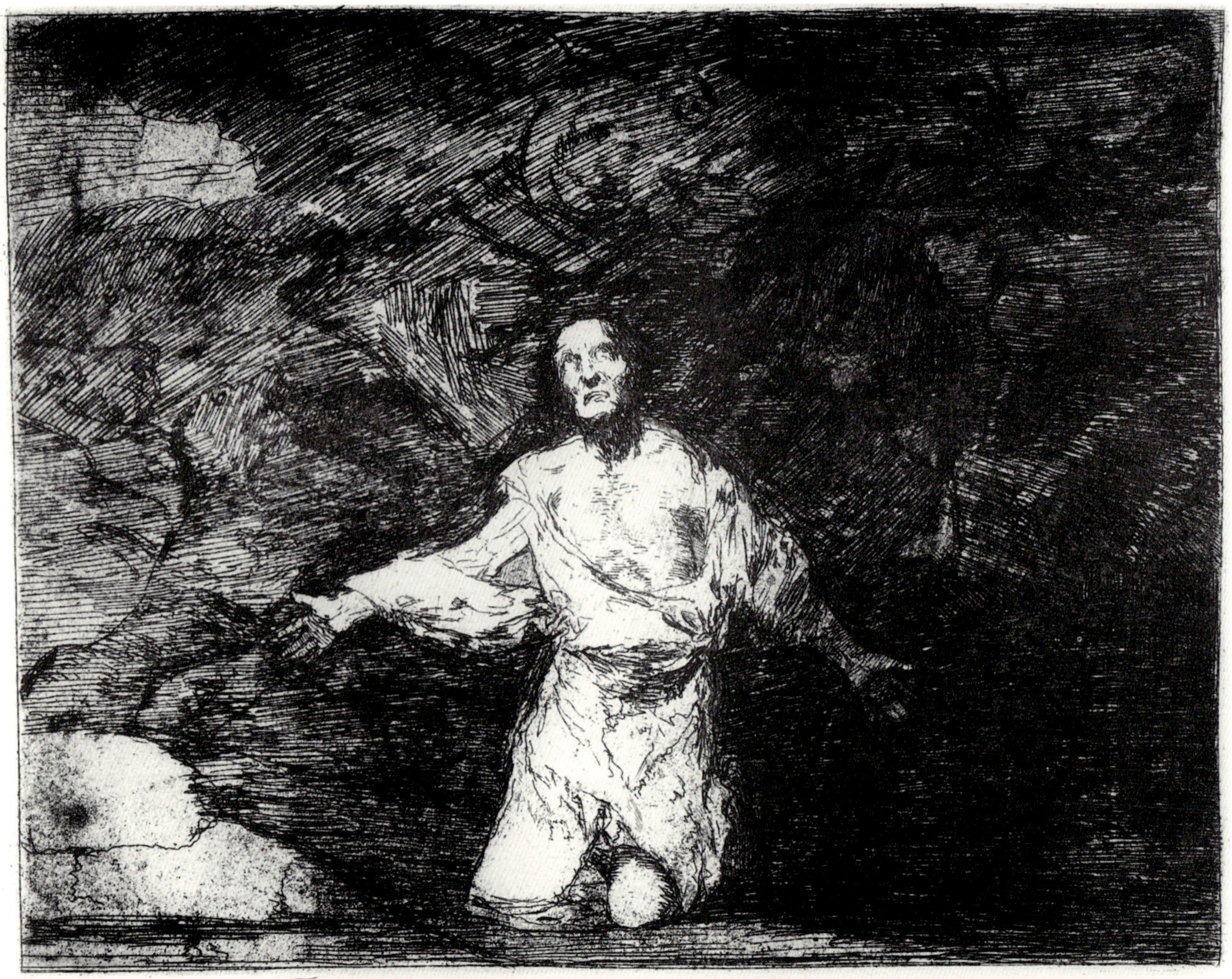

Tristes presentimientos de lo que ha de acontecer.

Plate 1

Dire forebodings of what is going to happen

etching and aquatint to a point that has rarely been surpassed. Yet, in *The Disasters of War,* etched in the early nineteenth century, Goya abandoned the subtleties and perfection of an essentially eighteenth-century manner for a much more direct and less polished way of making his statement about the barbarity of war.

The eighty-two etchings made for Goya's series were never published in his lifetime. He gave to his friend Juan Agustín Ceán Bermúdez a complete, bound set of the prints with captions written by him as a guide for a professional engraver (the album is now one of the British Museum's most prized possessions). The captions suggest that Goya must have intended to publish the prints, probably during or soon after the war, as a homage to the Spanish resistance and an inspiration to his fellow countrymen. Two of Goya's greatest paintings in the Prado show the popular uprising of the *Dos de mayo,* the second of May 1808 in Madrid, and its aftermath in the immortal scene of the *Tres de mayo,* the mass execution of Spanish patriots and innocent civilians by French troops the following night. These huge canvases were painted after the war was over, in 1815, but Goya began work on his prints in 1810, the date that appears on some of the earliest, signed copperplates in the series (plates 22 and 27).

The series depicts the horrors that resulted from the Napoleonic invasion of Spain. Napoleon Bonaparte's aim was to bring Spain within the orbit of his Empire, and to this end he planned to install his brother Joseph as its new monarch. However, he failed to reckon with the strength of Spanish patriotism and his generals met with violent and heroic attempts to expel the foreign troops and restore to the throne Ferdinand VII, the hereditary monarch who had been lured into exile in France. Goya's original title for the series was: *Fatal consequences of the bloody war in Spain with Bonaparte.* The initial inspiration may have been the journey that Goya made to Saragossa in the early stages of the war. Aragon was one of the most fiercely defended provinces, with an active guerrilla opposition to Napoleon's armies. In the summer of 1808, the French laid siege to the provincial capital Saragossa whose defence was brilliantly led by General Palafox. He succeeded in repelling the French forces, and immediately invited Goya to come and see for himself and record the devastation suffered by the city and its inhabitants. Goya made the long and dangerous journey across country to Saragossa that autumn, but was forced to leave the city when the French returned to set up a second siege. He spent the rest of the war in Madrid, no doubt following the news reports as they reached the capital and witnessing at first hand the terrible 'year of the famine' in 1811-1812, when 20,000 of the city's inhabitants died of starvation. Although Goya never worked directly for the 'Intruder

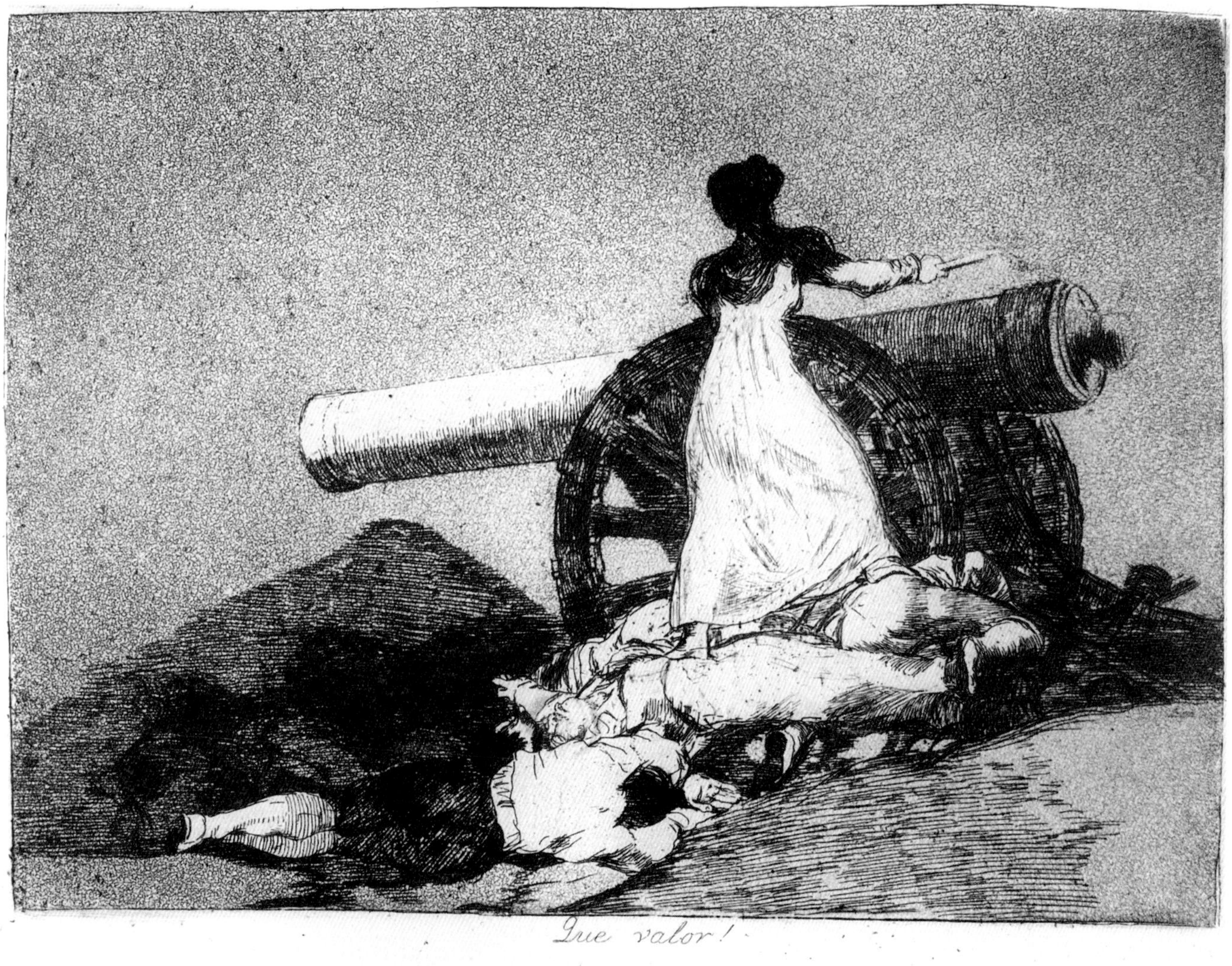

Plate 7
What courage!

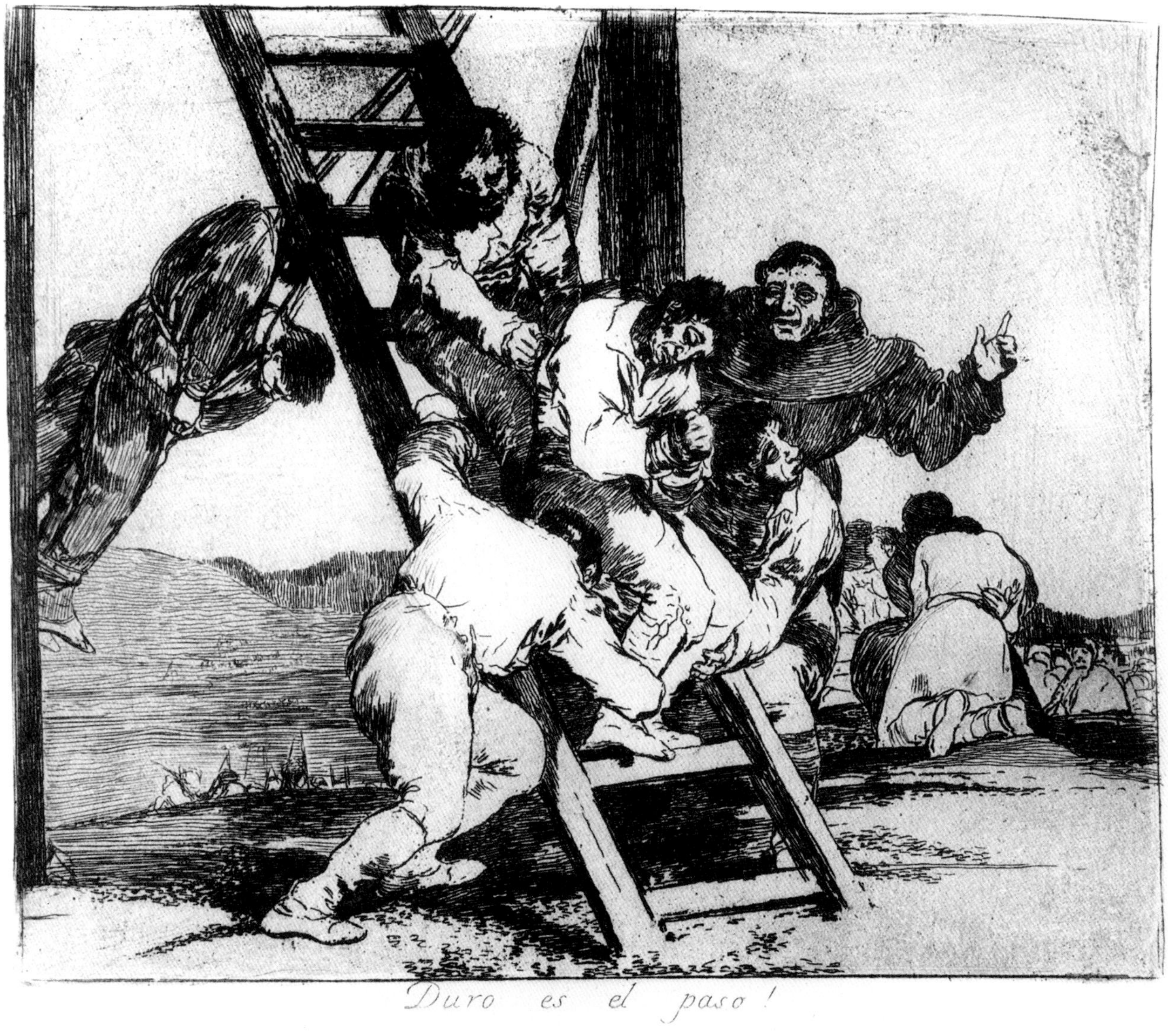

Plate 14
Hard is the way!

King', as Joseph Bonaparte was known, and did not draw his pay during the war, he continued his career as an official court artist, painting portraits of French generals and figures connected with the new régime. He kept his real views to himself and embarked on his set of prints as a personal response to the events of the war.

In 1863, years after Goya's death, the Royal Academy of Fine Arts in Madrid published eighty of Goya's prints with the title *Los Desastres de la guerra.* They fall into three principal groups: scenes of the war that had begun in 1808, of the famine in Madrid in 1811-12, and some allegorical subjects that were the latest to be etched. The most substantial group is concerned with the war and its effects, and the earliest prints (which are not arranged in the sequence in which they were made) are those that are signed and sometimes dated 1810 (plates 18, 22 and 27). They are characterised by relatively small-scale figures in open landscape settings, and they show the horrors faced by the civilian population after a battle: bodies, often stripped of their clothing, strewn over the ground and finally tipped into a common grave or simply a ravine. Goya's sympathies were directly engaged, as is seen in a plate to which he gave the title *I saw this* (plate 44). It shows terrified villagers fleeing from a still invisible enemy, with a fat parish priest in the vanguard, clearly unwilling to do anything to help the young mother struggling with her baby and a child - a reminiscence of the ironic, satirical vein in the earlier prints of *Los Caprichos.*

Goya's strong motivation, his overwhelming desire to create this series of war scenes, is strikingly demonstrated by four prints that he made on the backs of two of his most beautiful etchings, large landscapes with aquatint from which he had pulled only a few proofs. Desperately short of materials in Madrid, due to the fact that everything was turned to use for the war, he cut each copperplate in half, destroying his landscapes for ever, and etched four harrowing scenes on their versos, including the extraordinary image of the falling figures in their shattered home (plates 13, 14, 15 and 30). Goya made preparatory drawings for his prints, transferring them on to the copperplates as a guide for his etching needle. But as he advanced in the series, his hand and eye gained in assurance and he began to use a broader, more expressive style, limiting the preparatory drawings to a summary indication of the composition and often making radical changes as he worked out the design on the plate. (Almost all the preparatory drawings for Goya's prints are preserved in the Prado.)

The subjects of the prints fall into several categories of which one of the most impressive is Goya's presentation of Spanish women, the wives and mothers who fought 'like wild beasts' (plate 5) to resist rape and slaughter or who, like the heroic

Agustina of Aragon, fired a cannon when those who manned it had all fallen to the ground (plate 7): Goya does not name her - her deed was legendary and celebrated in many popular prints - but comments simply: 'What courage!'. His manuscript captions on the unique bound volume were faithfully transcribed on to the copperplates as published by the Academy. They are brief, the sort of outraged, despairing or ironic comments that the artist might have made as he watched a friend turn the pages of his prints: 'And there's nothing one can do about it' (plate 15), 'One can't watch this' (plate 26), 'Why?' (plate 32), 'Barbarians!' (plate 38) or the ironic 'What a feat! With dead men!' (plate 39). Although Goya was passionately patriotic, he does not overtly take sides. The dead are unidentified; the fate of French soldiers at the hands of the Spanish is evoked with the same sense of pity as he expresses for his countrymen (plate 16). In the famine scenes, Goya shows a plump Spanish girl walking past a group of starving people, including a famished, skeletal child, on her way to a rendezvous with a foreign soldier (plate 55), leaving it to the viewer to draw the conclusion.

It is the cruelty within all human nature, the instinct for survival, the desire for dignity and the betrayal of a people's sense of its own humanity that Goya reveals in this extraordinary series of prints. He makes use of every kind of etching technique, from the most delicate effects of line heightened by thin washes of acid in the early plates to rich, dramatic aquatints in many of the later famine scenes (plates 50 and 51). It is enlightening to compare the latter, full of subtle, original effects, with the inexpressive, mechanical aquatint grain that was added posthumously to plate 7, to conceal a number of defects in the background before publication. Perhaps the finest examples of his mature use of the etched line in combination with aquatint are found in the terrifying series of plates devoted to atrocities and summary executions (plates 32-39). Drawing on a store of images rooted in classical antiquity and the Italian masters, Goya presents almost symbolic images of war. Men hanged, shot, tortured and dismembered are seen in compositions structured as surely as the greatest masterpieces in oils. Naked torsos and limbs that evoke antique marble fragments - a reminiscence of his Roman stay - are combined with blasted trees and distant evocations of more horrors to come. The economy of Goya's line and the sober reticence of expression in these terrible scenes serve to make these images all the more telling.

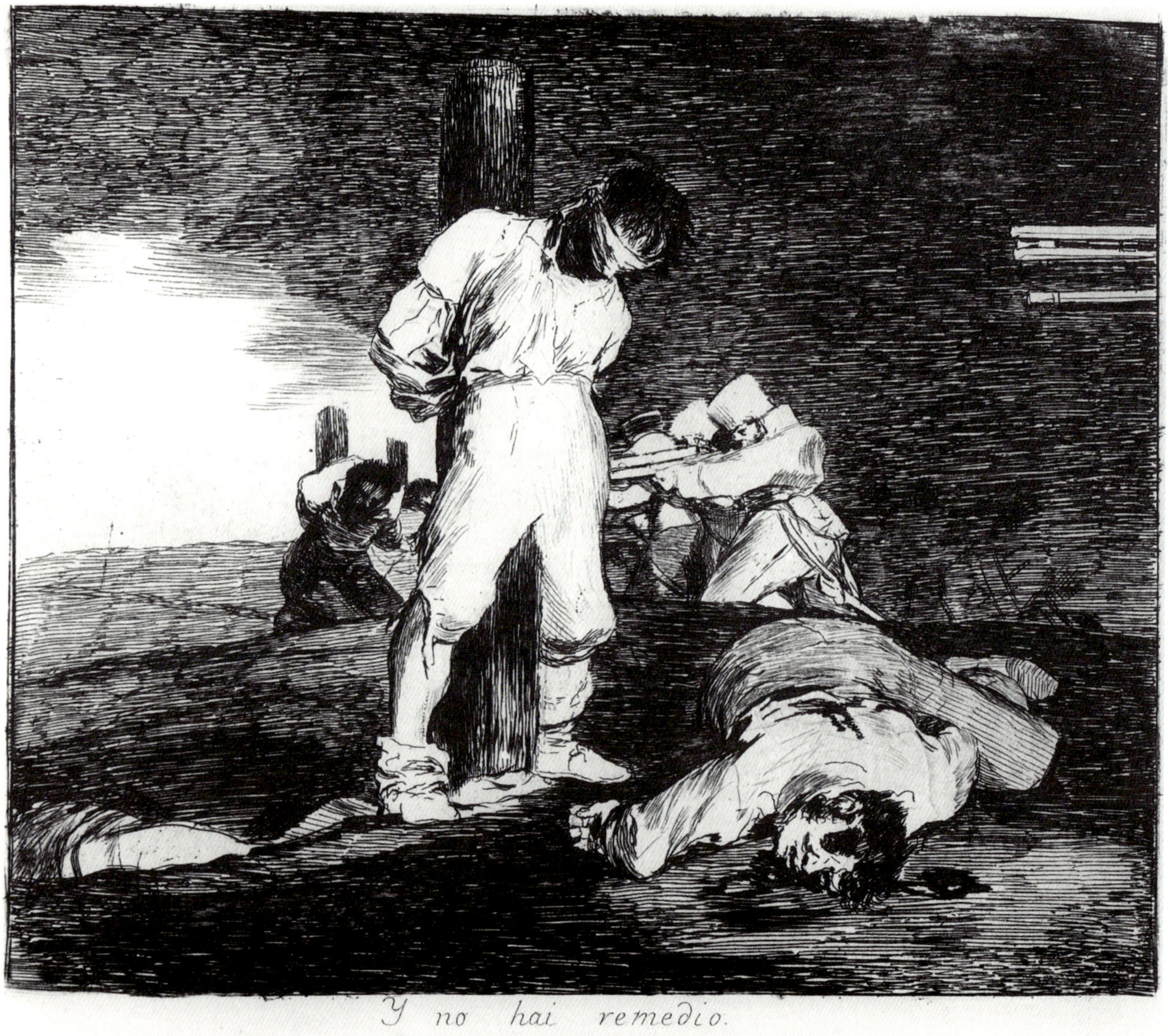

Plate 15

And there's nothing one can do about it

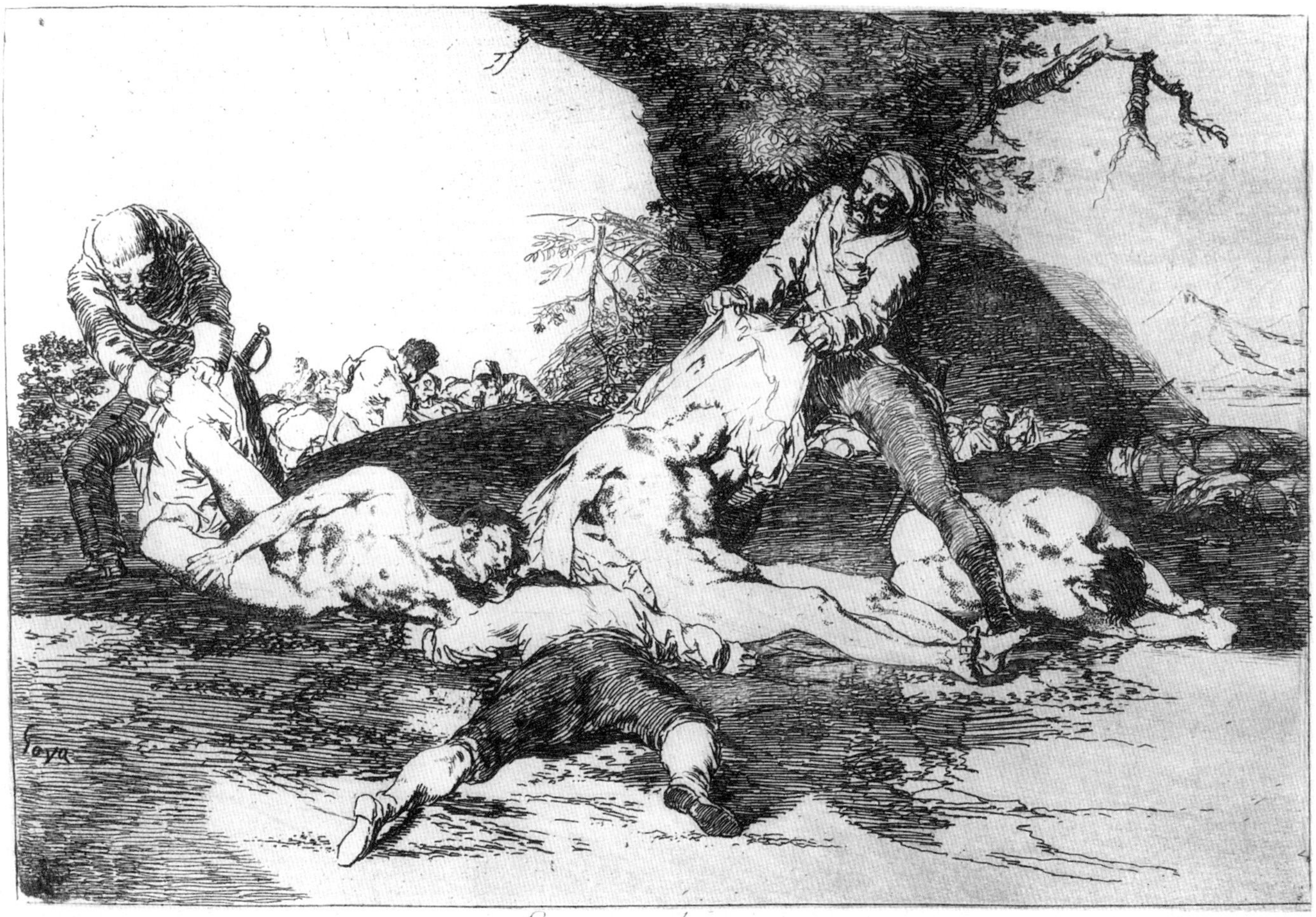

Se aprovechan.

Plate 16
They help themselves

Goya went on to complete his war and famine scenes with a group of strange allegorical 'caprichos'. These lie outside the images of the war itself, but one such later plate was designed as a frontispiece to the whole set (plate 1). Before moving into this final chapter - a return to the *Caprichos* through which he had expressed his earlier opposition to ignorance, curelty and oppression - Goya designed a print probably intended to complete his series on the war. Its original title was so inescapably pessimistic that the Royal Academicians felt obliged to alter its meaning. In place of Goya's manuscript: *Nada. Ello lo dice - Nothing. That's what he is saying* - the Academy substituted, in the engraved version, *Ello dirá - Time will tell* or *We shall see* (plate 69).

The return to Spain of Ferdinand 'the Desired', an intolerant bigot who seized absolute power, brought with it the overthow of all liberal ideals and aspirations and made it impossible for Goya to publish his reflections on the war and its aftermath. However, his will to create never left him, and he completed a new set of prints on bullfighting in 1816, while another planned series of large allegorical prints, which he entitled *Disparates,* was only abandoned when he left Spain for voluntary exile in France. When the Spanish Academy of Fine Arts published Goya's *The Disasters of War* in 1863, it restored to the world a work whose message is timeless and universal, and whose relevance is as strong today as it was in the circumstances of his time.

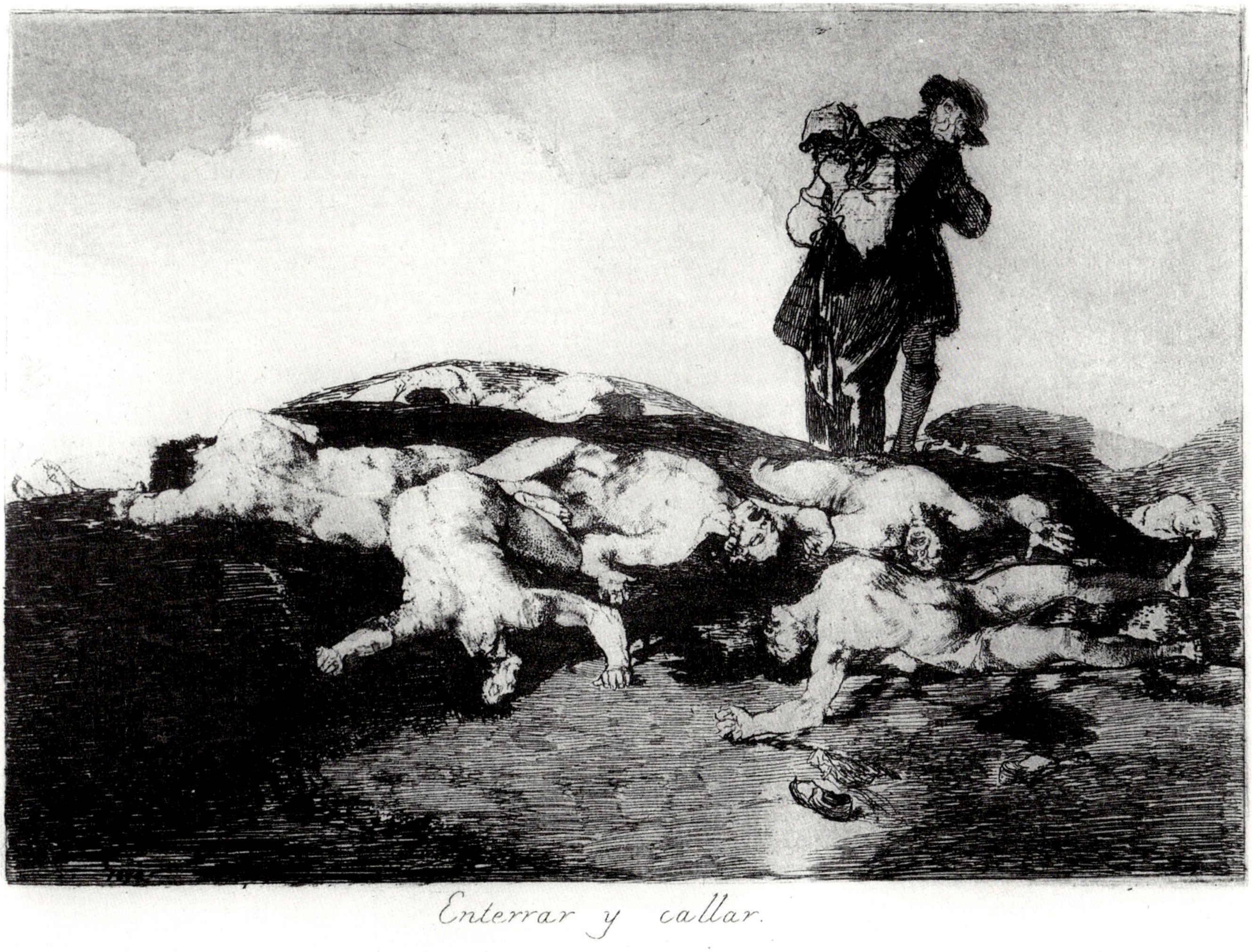

Plate 18

Bury them, without a word

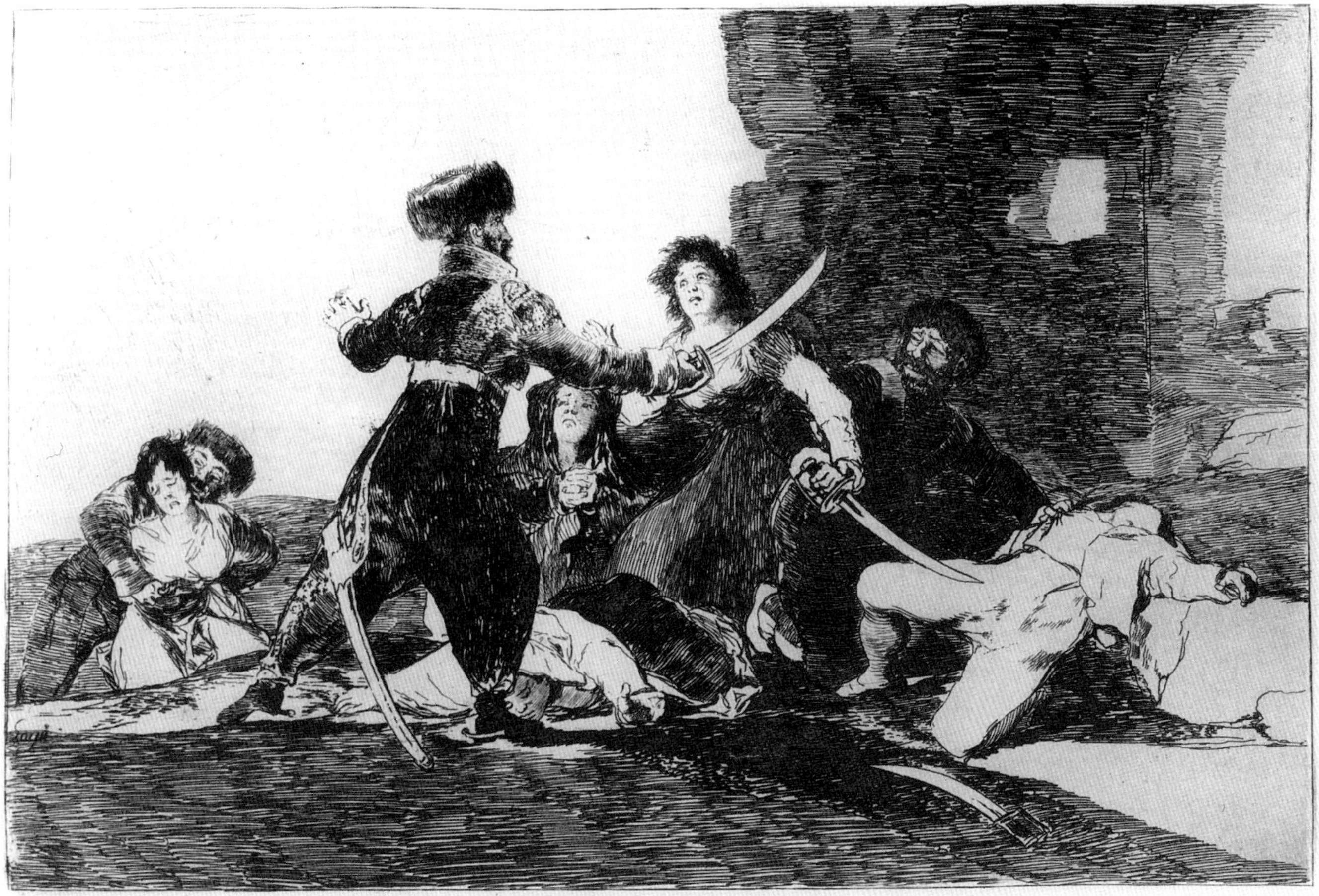

Ya no hay tiempo

Plate 19
It's already too late

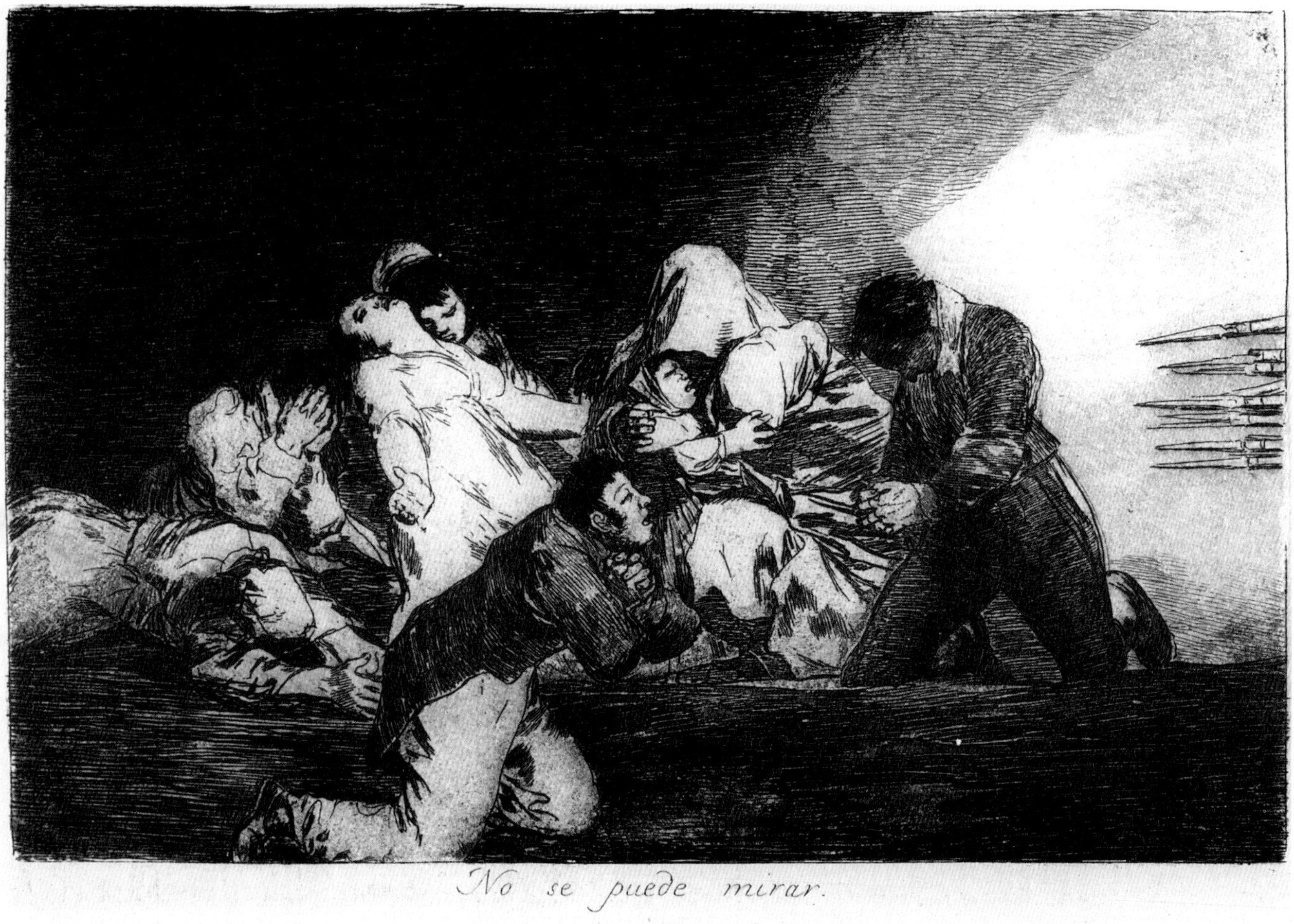

Plate 26

One can't watch this

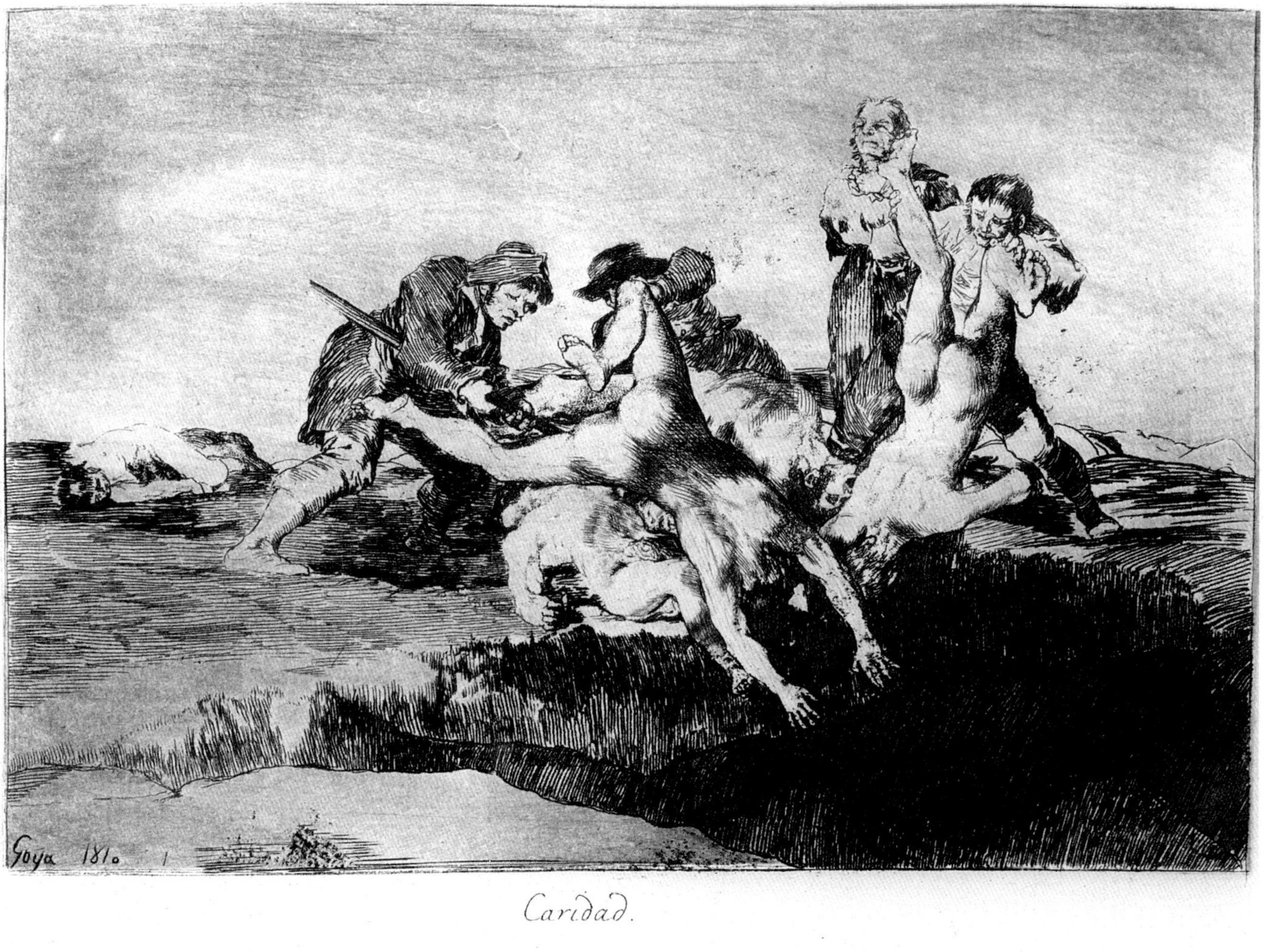

Plate 27
Charity

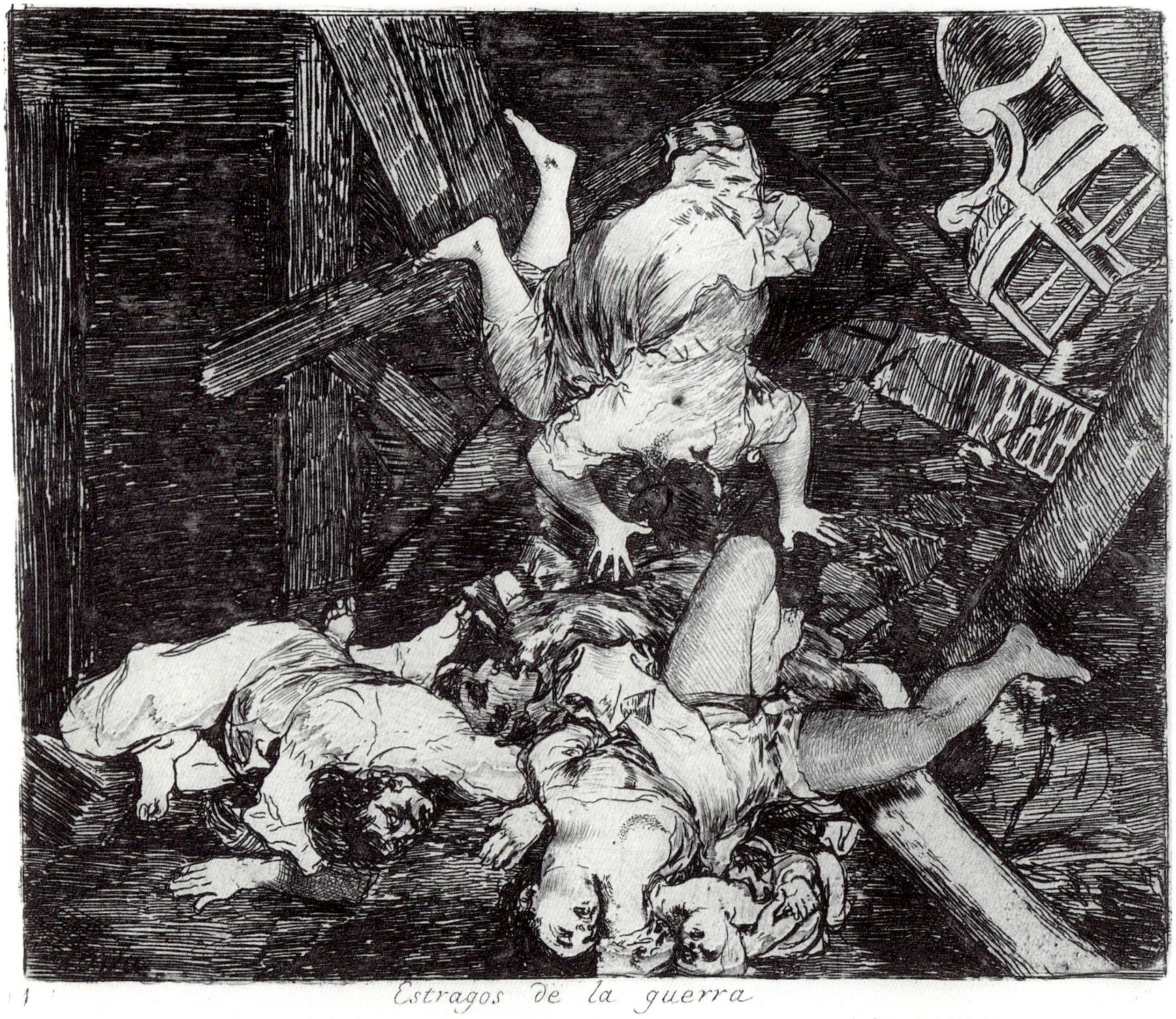

Plate 30
Ravages of war

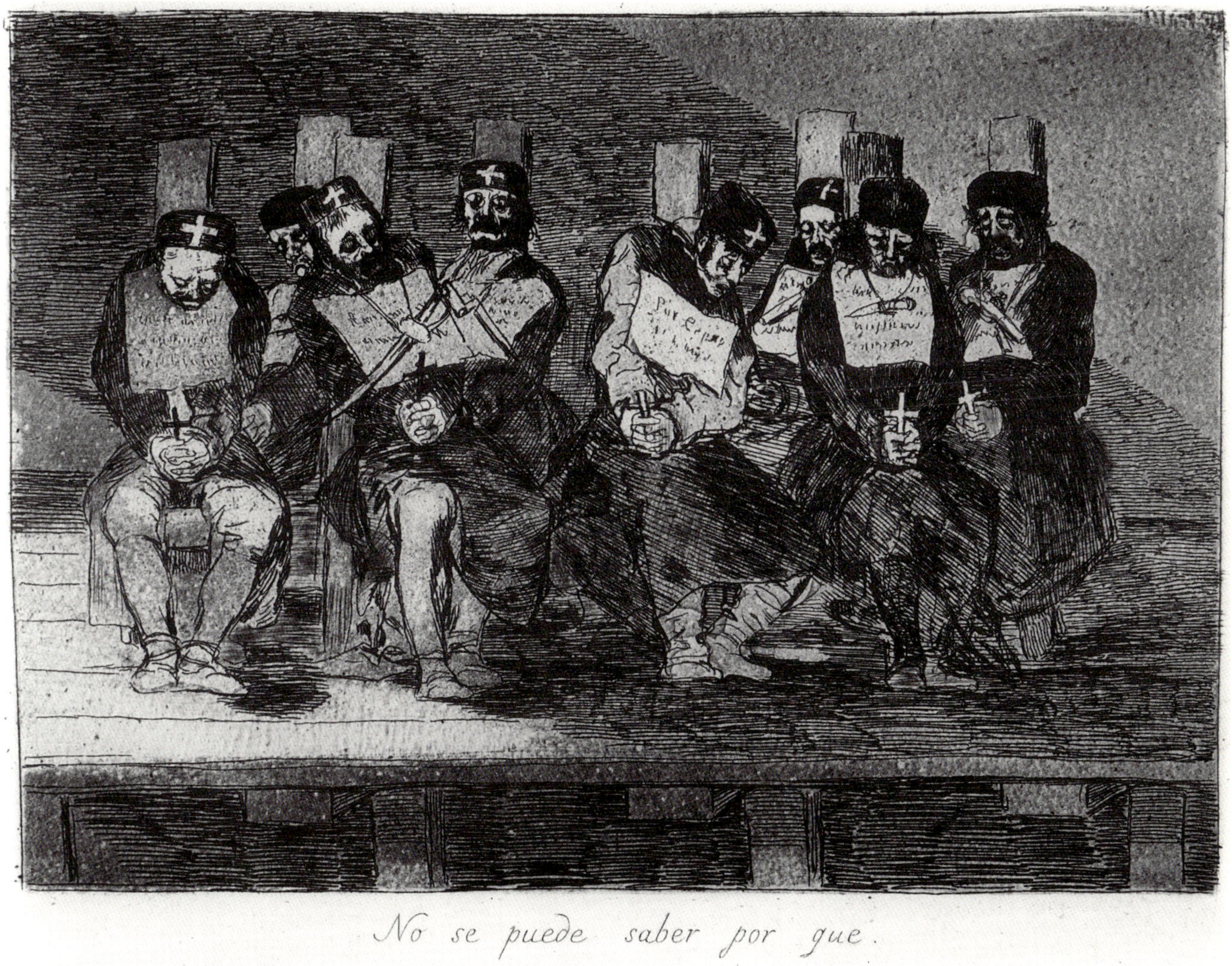

Plate 35
One can't tell why

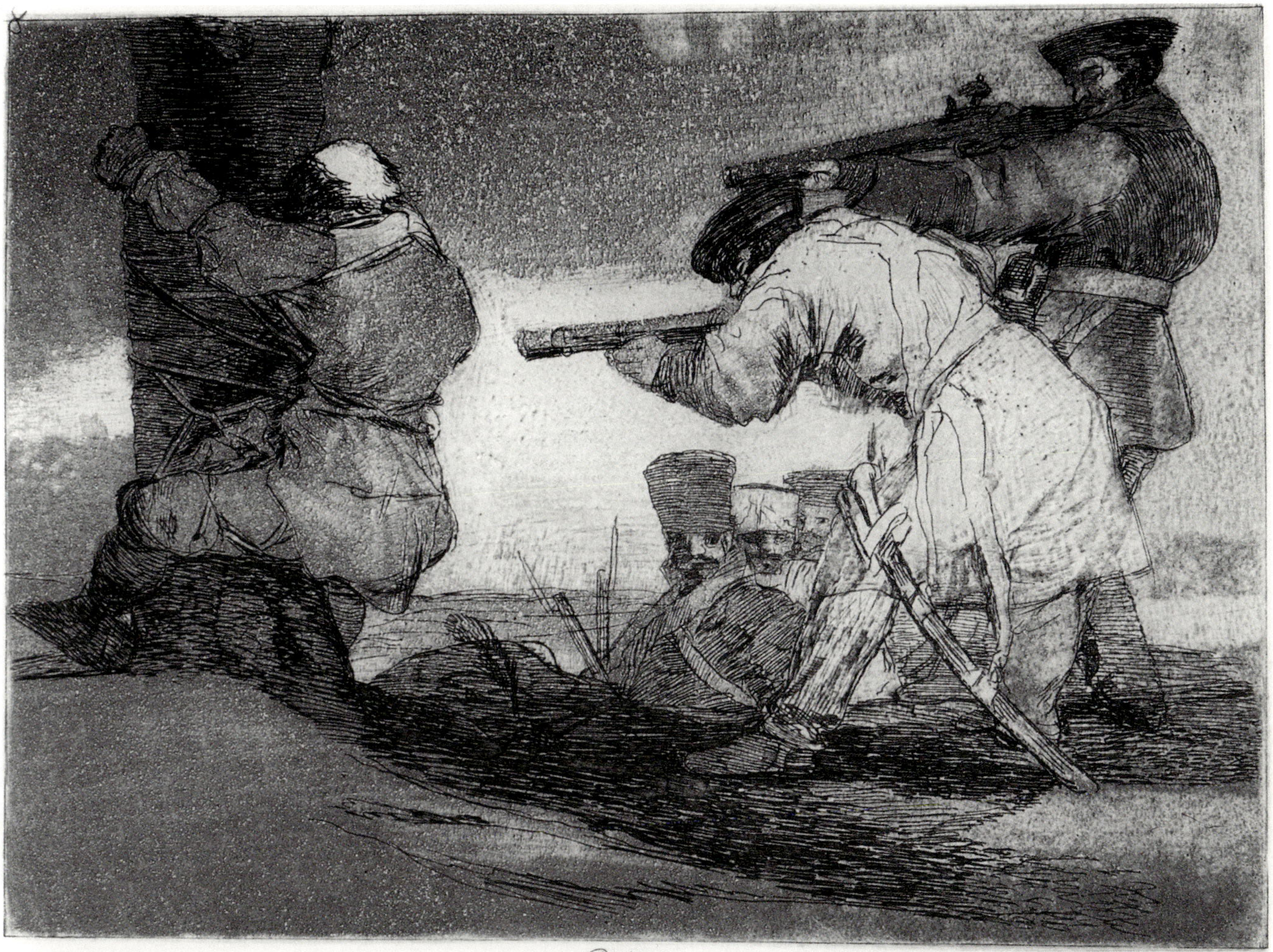

Bárbaros!

Plate 38
Barbarians!

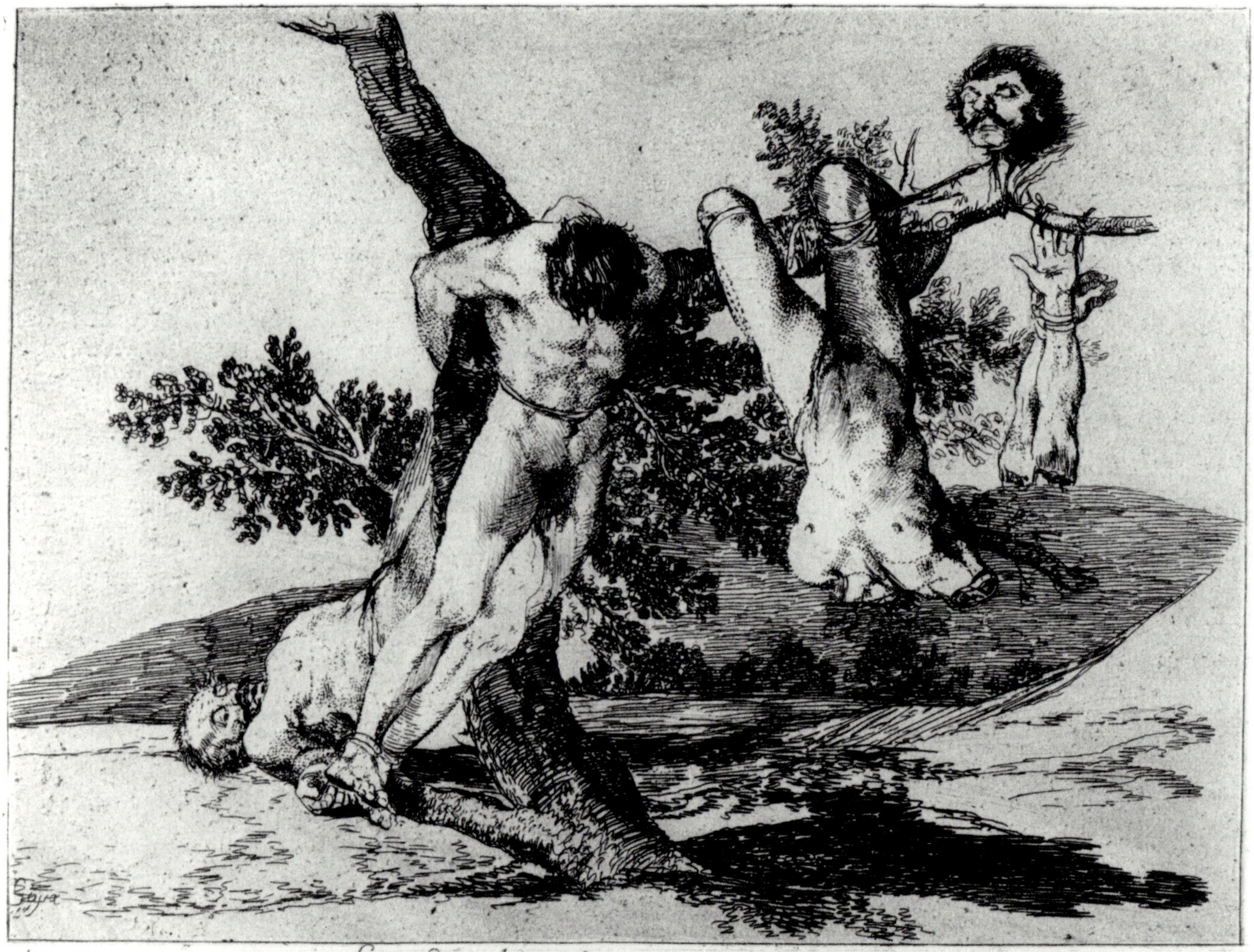

Grande hazaña. con muertos.

Plate 39
What a feat! With dead men!

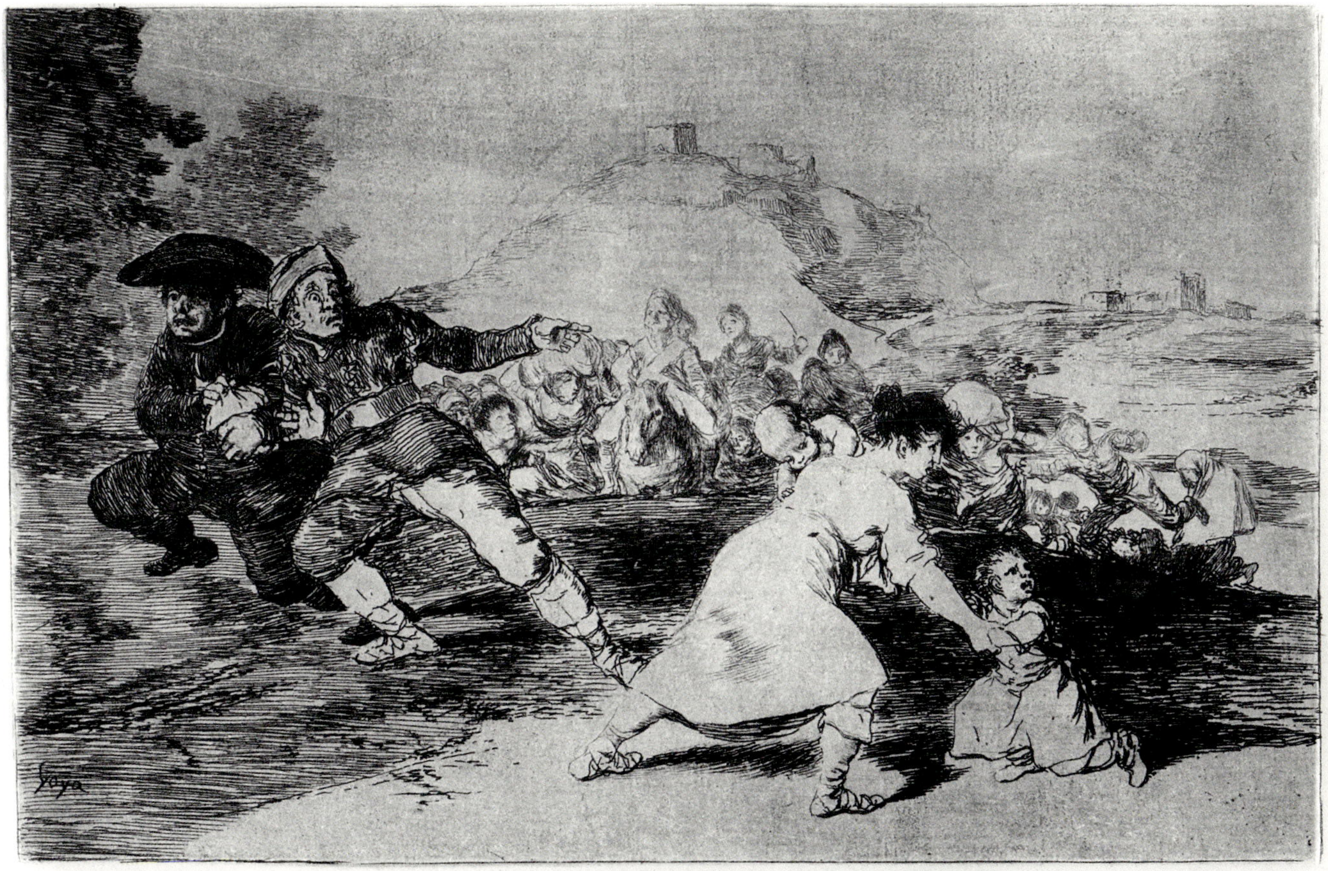

Yo lo vi.

Plate 44
I saw this

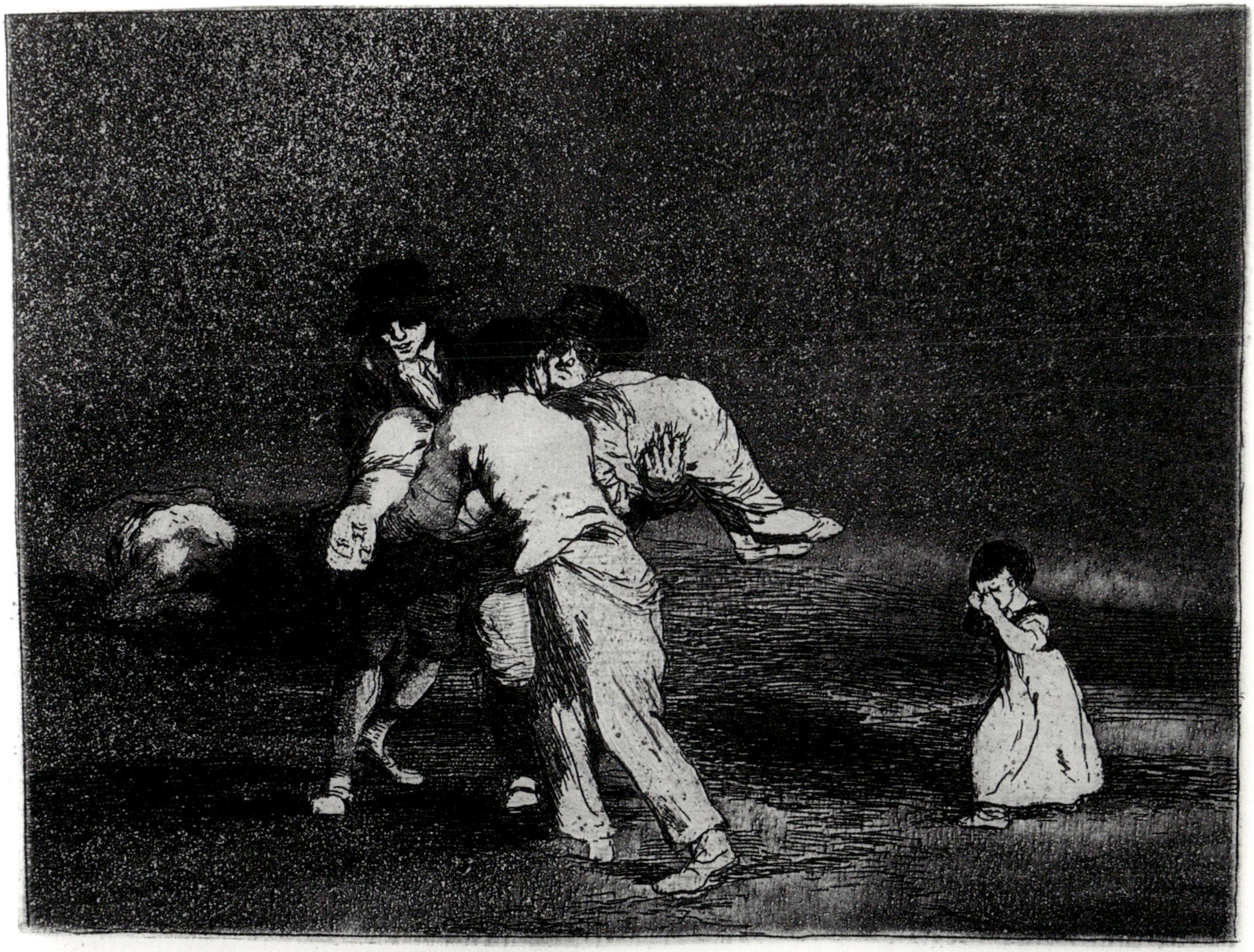

Madre infeliz!

Plate 50
Wretched mother!

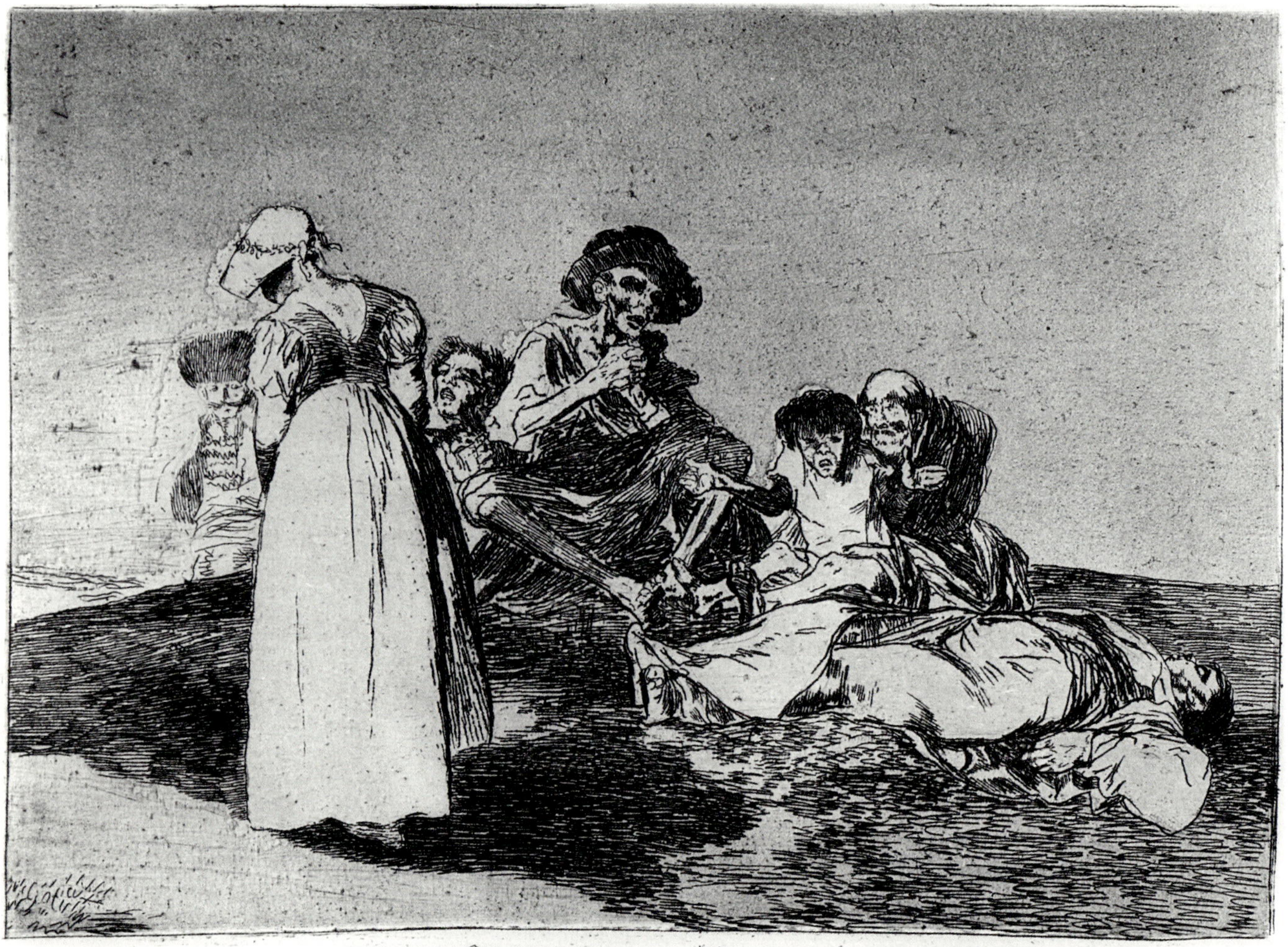

Lo peor es pedir

Plate 55

The worst is to beg

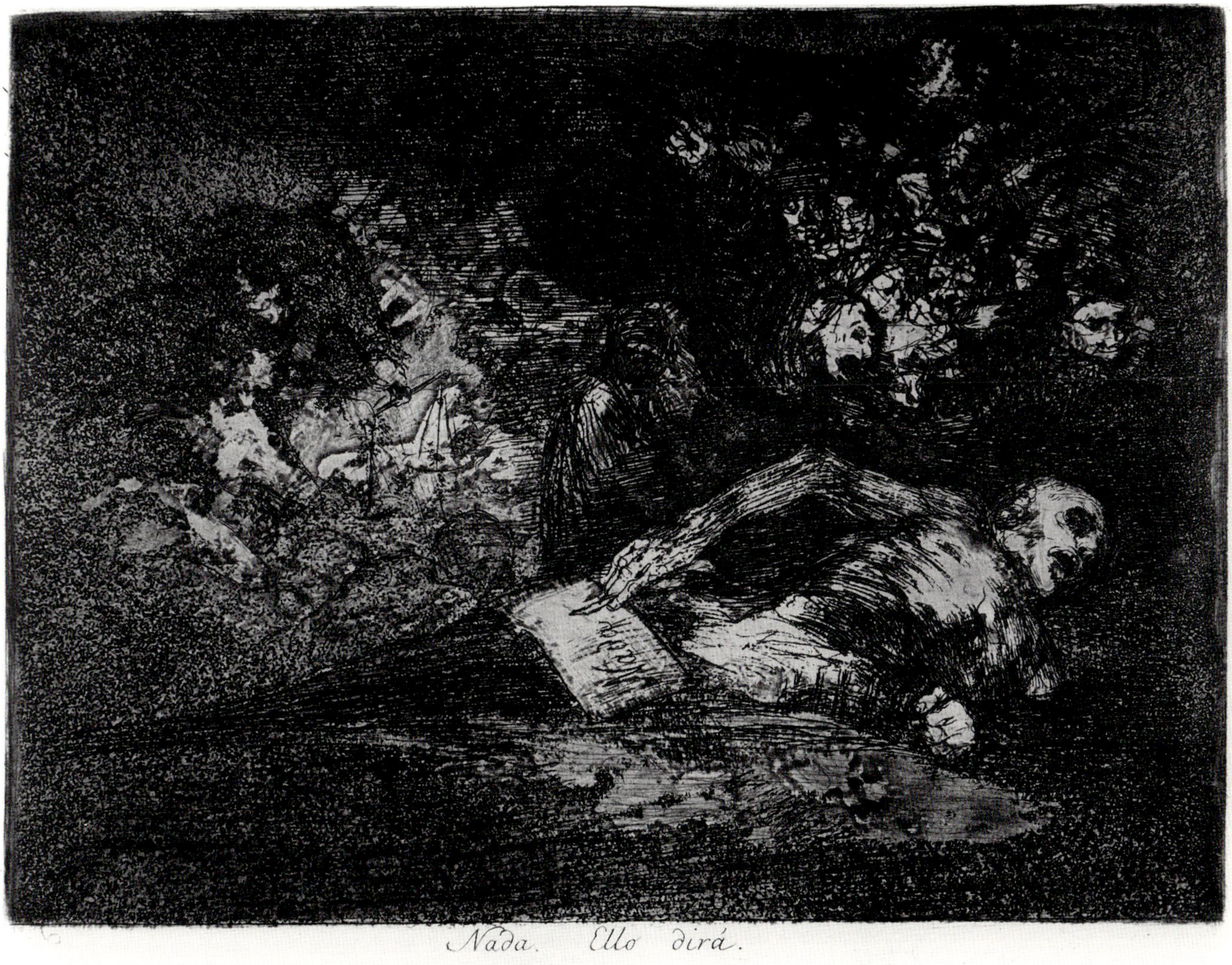

Plate 69

Nothing. Time will tell

Dix

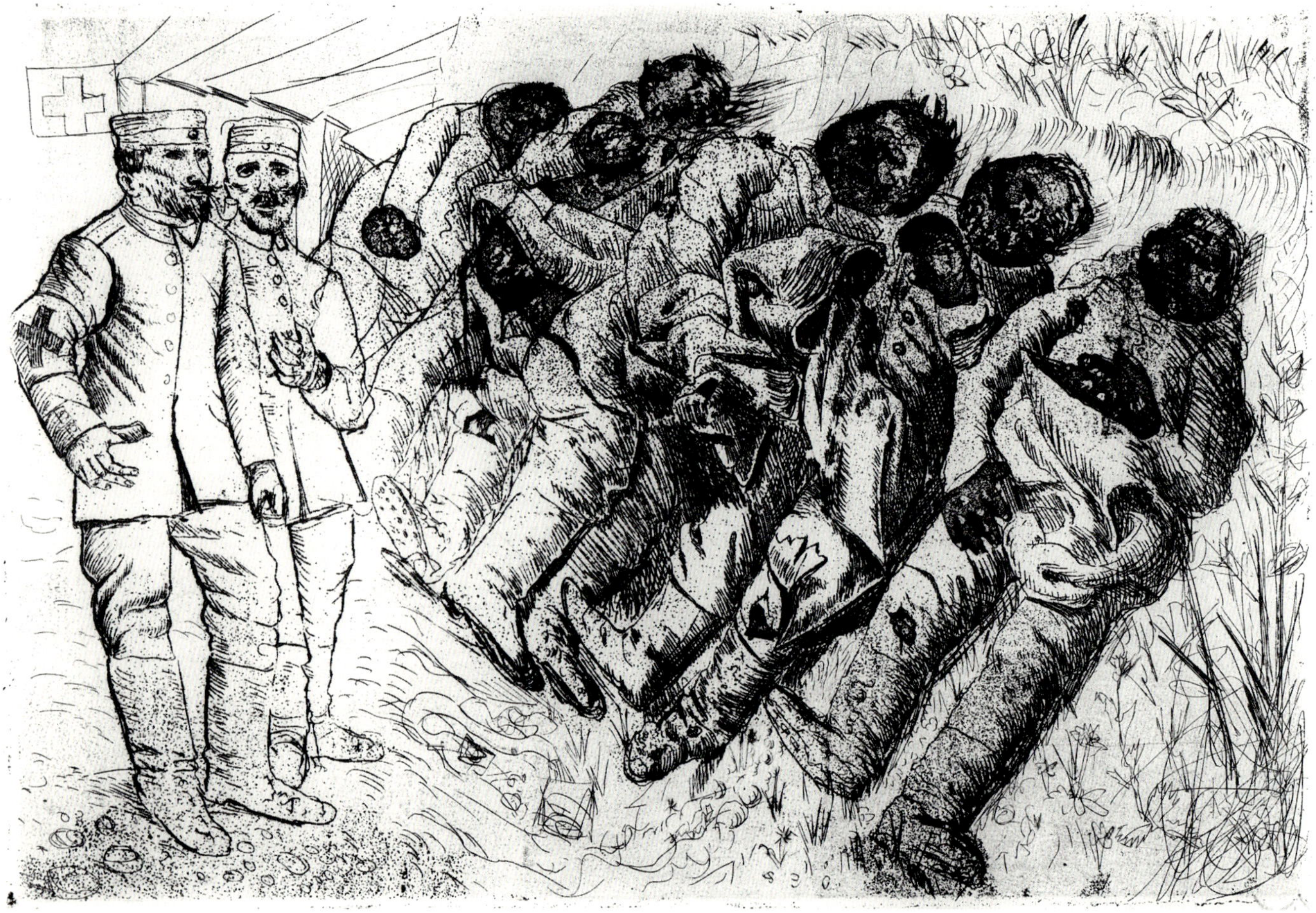

Plate 3
Men killed by gas (Templeux-La-Fosse, August 1916)

Dix: War

John Willett

So long as the First World War lasted, there was little but his obsessive draughtsmanship to distinguish Otto Dix from other young Germans of his age and social background. He joined the artillery within weeks of its outbreak, fought as an infantryman in Champagne between autumn 1915 and mid-1916, then in the Battle of the Somme, then on the Russian front before it collapsed. Back on the Western front he may have been briefly at Verdun, and was certainly in the fighting around Ypres. He was wounded in the neck, was awarded the Iron Cross class 2 and worked his way up from ordinary machine-gunner to Lance-Sergeant. In 1918, not long before the war ended, he applied to become an airman and was sent back to Bautzen in Saxony for training. This left him at the age of 27 some sixty kilometres away from Dresden and his interrupted education as an artist.

Dix had taken into the army with him a passion for drawing in charcoal or soft black pencil, and the self-evident model for his violently black war drawings was the work of Umberto Boccioni and other Italian Futurists, a selection of whose pictures had been touring central Europe after their introduction by the Berlin 'Sturm' gallery in spring 1912; they were shown in Dresden, though opinions differ as to whether Dix saw them. He made hundreds of such drawings - many of them on postcards - during his service in France, Russia and Flanders, showing the destruction of villages, trees and trench systems, the upturning of fields by shellfire, the savage confusion of hand-to-hand fighting, the vast rushing of projectiles, men and vehicles, all in terms of those Futurist conventions of overlapping shapes and quasi-rayonist 'lines of force' which stemmed from Marinetti's protofascist dynamism.

There is a superficially similar chopping-up of the war landscape on Futurist lines in the work of August Stramm, the outstanding poet of *Der Sturm*, whose dissection of language springs from the same modernist technique; thus 'Shrapnel':

> The sky casts clouds
> Crackling into smoke.
> Jagged lightning.
> Feet shift pebble spray.
> Eyes titter at tangle
> And
> Slope off.

But what seems to set Dix's on-the-spot sketches of front-line feelings and experience so puzzingly apart from his mature war etchings of 1923-24 is not so much a Nietzschean, Dionysiac urge to participate, or even their Futurist echoes, as their almost complete absence of living persons. Often there are no faces to such figures as he includes there; at best they show a stereotyped set of snarling teeth; it is as if the artist dare not make them as lively as the torn-up soil.

For many of Dix's colleagues and contemporaries the violent traumas of the war changed their entire attitude, not only to the existing order in Germany, but also to the direction, style and technique of their own work. It is interesting how the two things went together. The Austrian cavalryman Oskar Kokoschka, after being badly wounded in the head, went to convalesce in Dresden, where he developed a rich new style of painting. Of the Brücke artists, Ernst Ludwig Kirchner broke down and settled in Switzerland; Max Pechstein was interned in Japan, then spent two years on the Western Front, made some remarkable etchings of the Battle of the Somme and returned to take a leading part in the post-war arts structure. Max Beckmann at first became a medical orderly and made some drawings on the Russian and Flanders fronts, but broke down in 1915 and was discharged to Frankfurt, where he abandoned his pre-war Impressionism to paint *Resurrection,* 1917/18 and *Night,* 1918-19 and embark on the socially critical graphics of *Die Hölle* and other series. Of Dix's Dresden contemporaries, George Grosz volunteered, broke down, was discharged, called up again, put in an asylum and rescued by Count Harry Kessler to work on a propaganda film. The young Conrad Felixmüller, who designed the cover for the Dresden magazine *Menschen* at the beginning of 1918, refused to be conscripted and was sent as a nurse to a military asylum, where he found that his charges were:

> ...all human like me. Flesh, bodies, bones - curious shapes,
> part soft, part hard. Pain everywhere, most of all in the head...

Plate 4
Field of shell craters near Dontrien lit up by flares

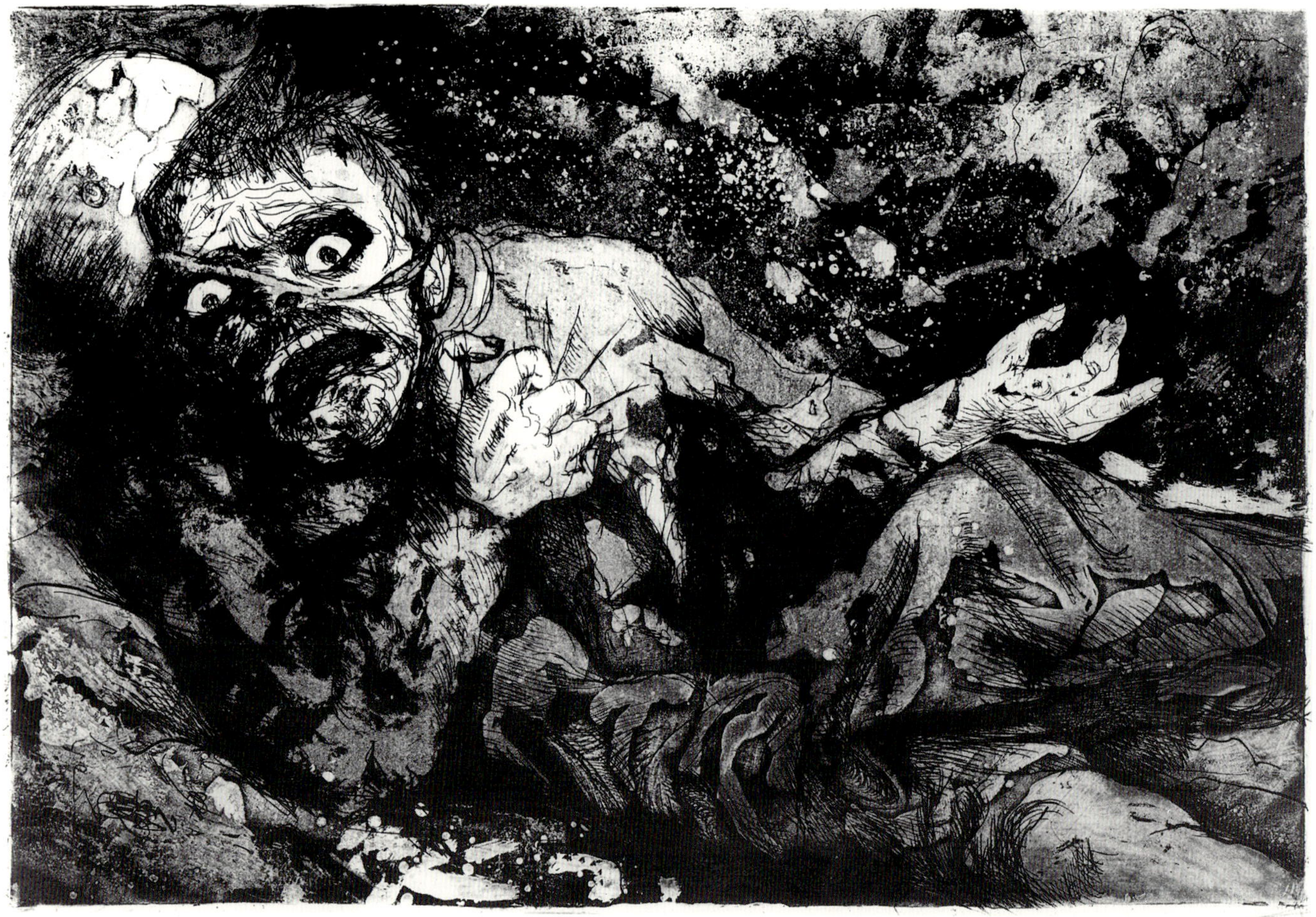

Plate 6
Wounded (Autumn 1916, Bapaume)

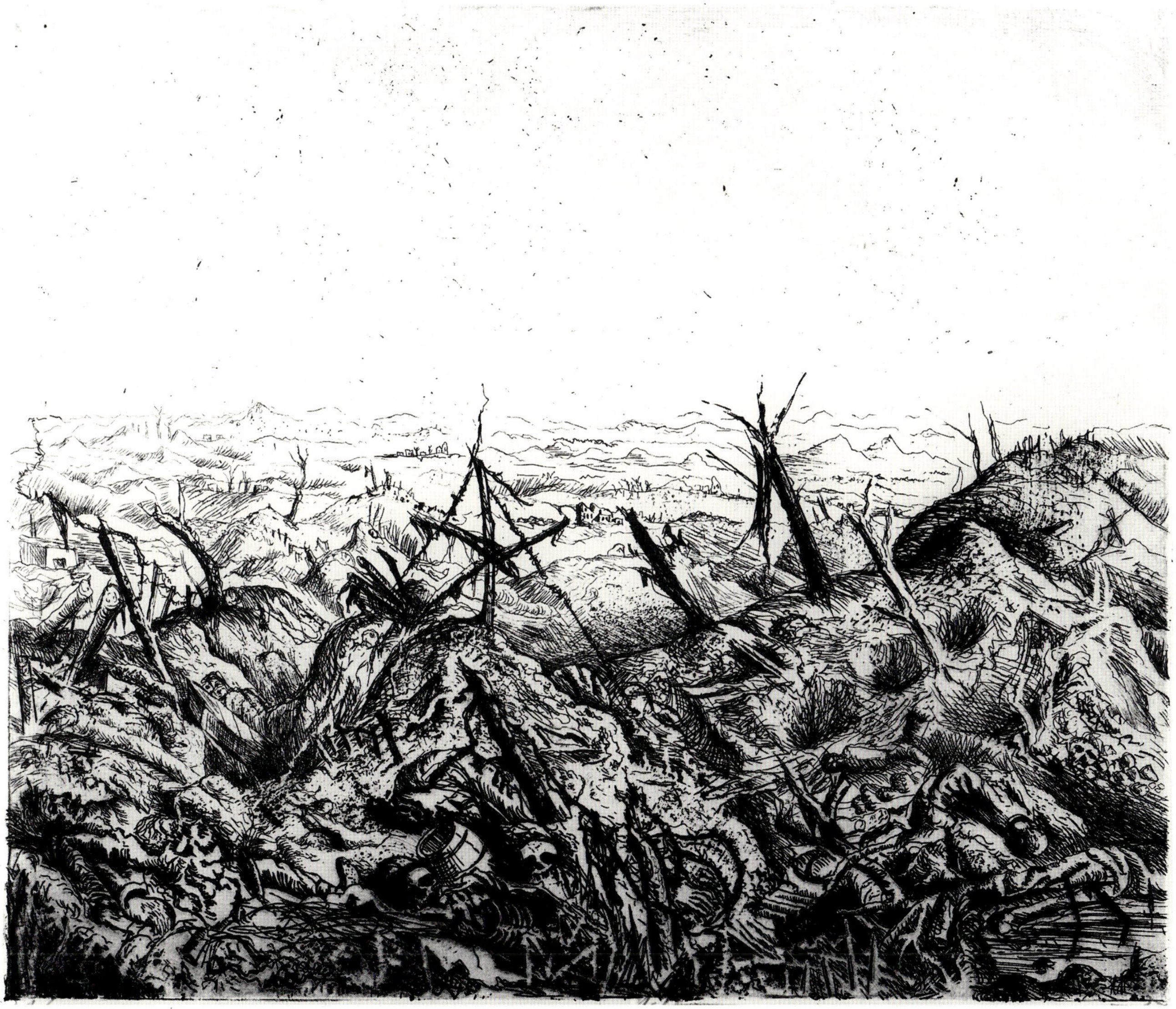

Plate 7
Near Langemark

Back in the Dresden area as the war ended, Dix joined with Felixmüller, Otto Griebel, Otto Schubert and Lasar Segall to form the radical Gruppe 1919 of the Dresden Sezession. Kokoschka, a professor at the Academy for the next four years, was an honorary member. There are paintings or drawings where Dix, Felixmüller, Griebel and Karl Günther portray one another in various combinations. Meanwhile Dix applied to go back to art school as a student at the Academy, where he soon became a master pupil of Pechstein's former teacher Otto Gußmann, and was given a studio of his own. It was these two steps that launched Dix on his ambiguous new course of the early 1920s: pacifist and socially critical on the one hand, technically tradition-based on the other. For a very short while his post-war work seems like a development of his front-line drawings, with recognisably the same dynamism and Futurist simultaneity. Then his friends in the Group introduced him to the Berlin Dadaists, of whom Grosz and John Heartfield had joined the new Communist Party along with Felixmüller and Griebel, and from then on the Futurism was virtually forgotten; he found himself on a new and stimulating platform; a small Dresden Dada unit was formed, and the advanced critics paid attention to his work.

Like Grosz and the Karlsruhe Dadaist Rudolf Schlichter, Dix now launched his attack on the German social and military Establishment as it had emerged from the war: bemedalled ex-officers, upper and lower bourgeoisie, whores of almost unrelieved ugliness; and also beggars, war victims with artificial limbs, and worn-down workers of his own class. At first the angle was satirical; Dix used a collage technique derived from Cubism by the Dadaists and well suited to depicting those war wounded (as in *Prager Straße* and *The Skat Players* of 1920) whose limbs and other organs had been blown off and mechanically pinned together by army surgery. Then the Berlin 'Dada Club' headed by Grosz, Heartfield and Raoul Hausmann invited him to contribute in June 1920 to the First (and last) International Dada Fair which they staged in a private gallery in Berlin. Here, among some 170 other exhibits, there were three eye-catching contributions: Grosz's painting *Deutschland, ein Wintermärchen*, Dix's two-metre wide procession of *War Cripples* and, floating just below the ceiling, Schlichter's stuffed effigy of a German soldier with gas mask and a pig's head. 'If drawings could kill,' said Kurt Tucholsky, who contributed a short review to the *Weltbühne*, 'the Prussian military would long since have been dead'.

It was after the war, rather than during his front-line service, that Dix 'kept having these dreams where I had to crawl through demolished houses, through passages I could hardly get through. My dreams were full of débris'. According to an interview which he gave near the end of his life they recurred over a period of some ten years. And his first big, nearly eight foot-square painting of *The Trench*, 1920-23, did look (in contrast to those of his Dada period) like a desperate attempt not to satirise but to exorcise them in a classically academic style. He began this work of minutely detailed gruesomeness when he was still at the Dresden Academy, brought it with him to Düsseldorf in 1922, and sold the finished work in 1923 to the great Wallraf-Richartz Museum in Cologne. This caused a major art controversy, with Max Liebermann in favour of the picture and Julius Meier-Graefe and Cologne's mayor Konrad Adenauer against it, with the upshot that the picture was returned to Dix, who lent it to the travelling show called *Nie wieder Krieg!* or *Never another War!*. This pacifist exhibition was designed to mark the tenth anniversary of the outbreak of war. Clearly his new Berlin dealer Karl Nierendorf was conscious of the occasion, for he commissioned the artist of *The Trench* to make a series of fifty prints on the same theme, to be published in Berlin during 1924. The big picture itself was bought by Dresden State Art Gallery after the end of its tour, and put uncontroversially in the city's reserve collection, where the Nazis would confiscate it when Hitler came to power; it has since disappeared and was presumably destroyed. The prints - *Der Krieg* - have survived, to constitute Dix's finest, most famous and passionate work.

o

Dix's war etchings have been compared with Goya's *The Disasters of War*, which it seems the German artist had partly in mind. They were published by Nierendorf from the Lützowstraße in West Berlin in five linen-bound portfolios, each priced at 300 new (post-stabilisation) Marks, or 1000 Marks for the lot. A selection of twenty-four gravure reproductions by the same printer, Felsing of Berlin, was issued at the same time for 2 Mks 40 Pf. There were seventy sets of the complete work, of which only one was actually subscribed, thanks to the drastic currency reform which entirely disrupted the market for modern graphics; the sales of the cheap selection, however, must have run into the thousands. Fifteen hundred were ordered by the trade unions for their 'anti-war' day, and Nierendorf sent out some hundreds of copies to the press, leading writers and local branches of peace and human rights societies. 'There has never been a bigger campaign to sell a work in portfolio form', he told the artist.

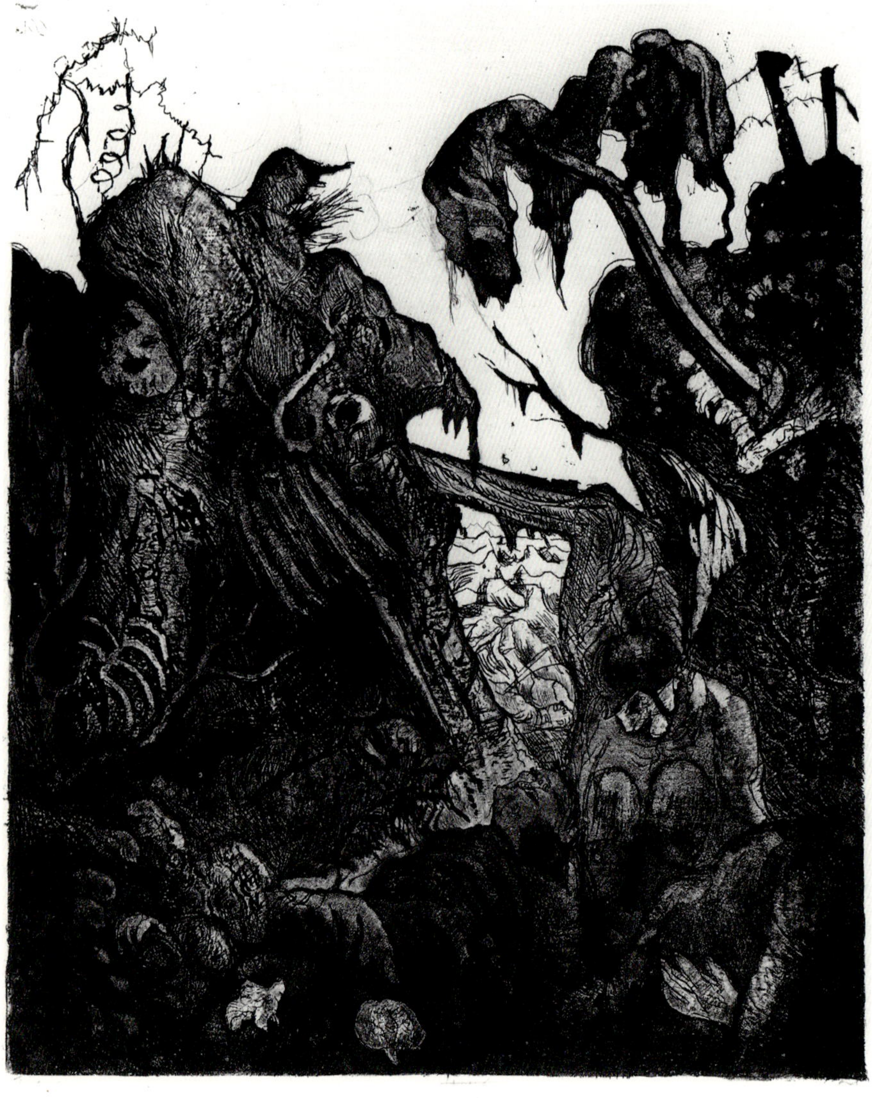

Plate 9
Destroyed trenches

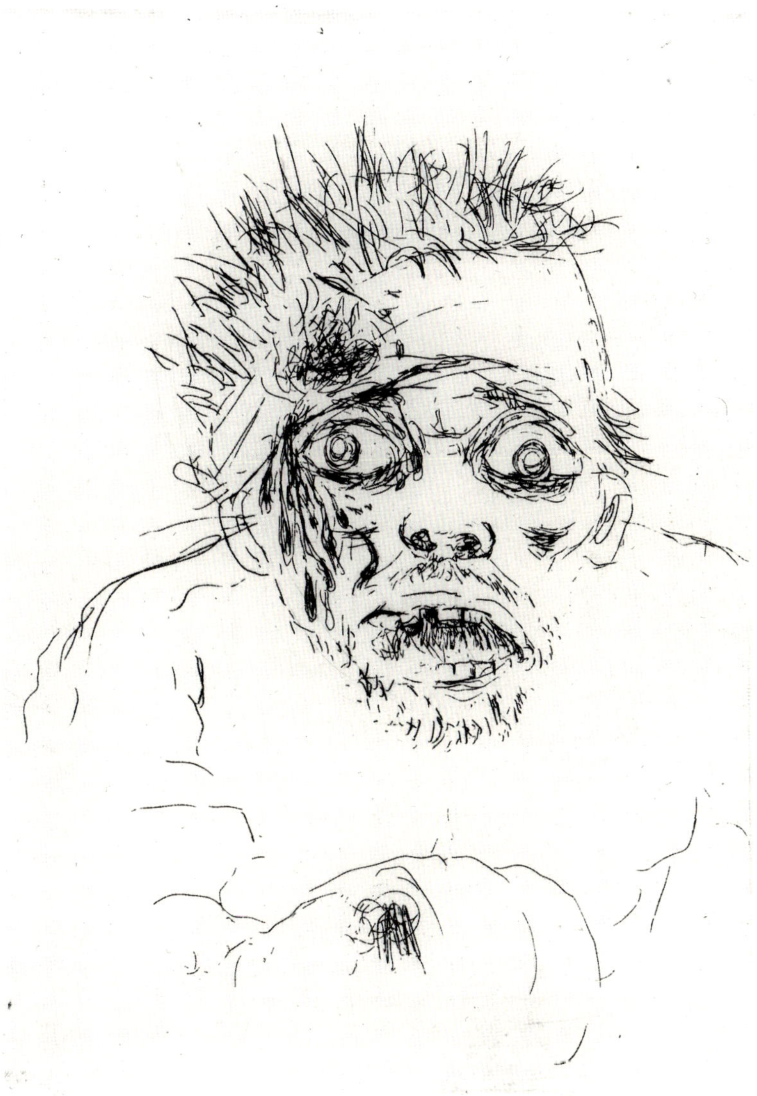

Plate 10
Fleeing wounded man (Battle of the Somme 1916)

Linked by their theme, the Western Front between 1916-1918, and by their technique, which is a mixture of etching and aquatint, the fifty prints are in other respects extremely varied. They seem to be presented in a random order, neither chronological, thematic nor topographic. Their plate sizes differ: sometimes they are in line on a white ground, sometimes on a tint, sometimes white areas are sharply bitten out of the drawing, sometimes the line is white on black. We see soldiers advancing, waiting, alone, in groups, in featureless gasmasks, in village brothels, lustful, looting, wounded, dead, skeletons and skulls. The shattered (and often shattering) scene switches irregularly between Champagne in 1916, the first battle of the Somme, Brussels, Antwerp, a Verdun fort, Mons, Tournai, Ypres. It is all very unlike the drawings in the wartime *Illustrated London News* or, for that matter, in *Krieg und Kunst*, the fortnightly instalments of lithographs by Lovis Corinth, Willy Jaeckel, Moriz Melzer and other artists of the Berlin Sezession which appeared from 1914 on. And as soon as you take them up - the actual prints, that is, rather than even the finest reproductions - you are conscious of having great works in your hands.

Given Dix's distortions and his ingrained love of the grotesque there was (and still is) a certain absurdity in pretending that his work was cool and objective in the spirit of Neue Sachlichkeit, let alone 'matter of fact' (which is perhaps the most literal translation of 'sachlich', and the best description of that mid-1920s movement). But within the field covered by the Mannheim exhibition of that name (which was toured to Dresden and five other mid-German cities) he was certainly on the more socially critical side. In 1926, after he had been in Berlin for some months, Nierendorf held an exhibition of Dix's portraits and launched a 'new club', the Society for Politics, Science and Art, which was like a successor to the Red Group. A week later, the dealer Alfred Flechtheim, who like Nierendorf had transferred his main effort from the Rhineland to Berlin, gave a show to Grosz, whose revolutionary impulse was already fading when the Red Group petered out. All in all, the particular kind of 'realism with a social flavour' which characterised the Mannheim exhibition not only brought Dix to prominence but formed the core of a particularly German form of 'Socialist Realism', sharper and more modern than the Russian brand, which would re-surface two decades later as the mainstream tradition of East German art. It shows perhaps how little an artist can determine what impact his work is going to make; its energy and originality are in the pictures; they do not necessarily stem from his conscious will.

o

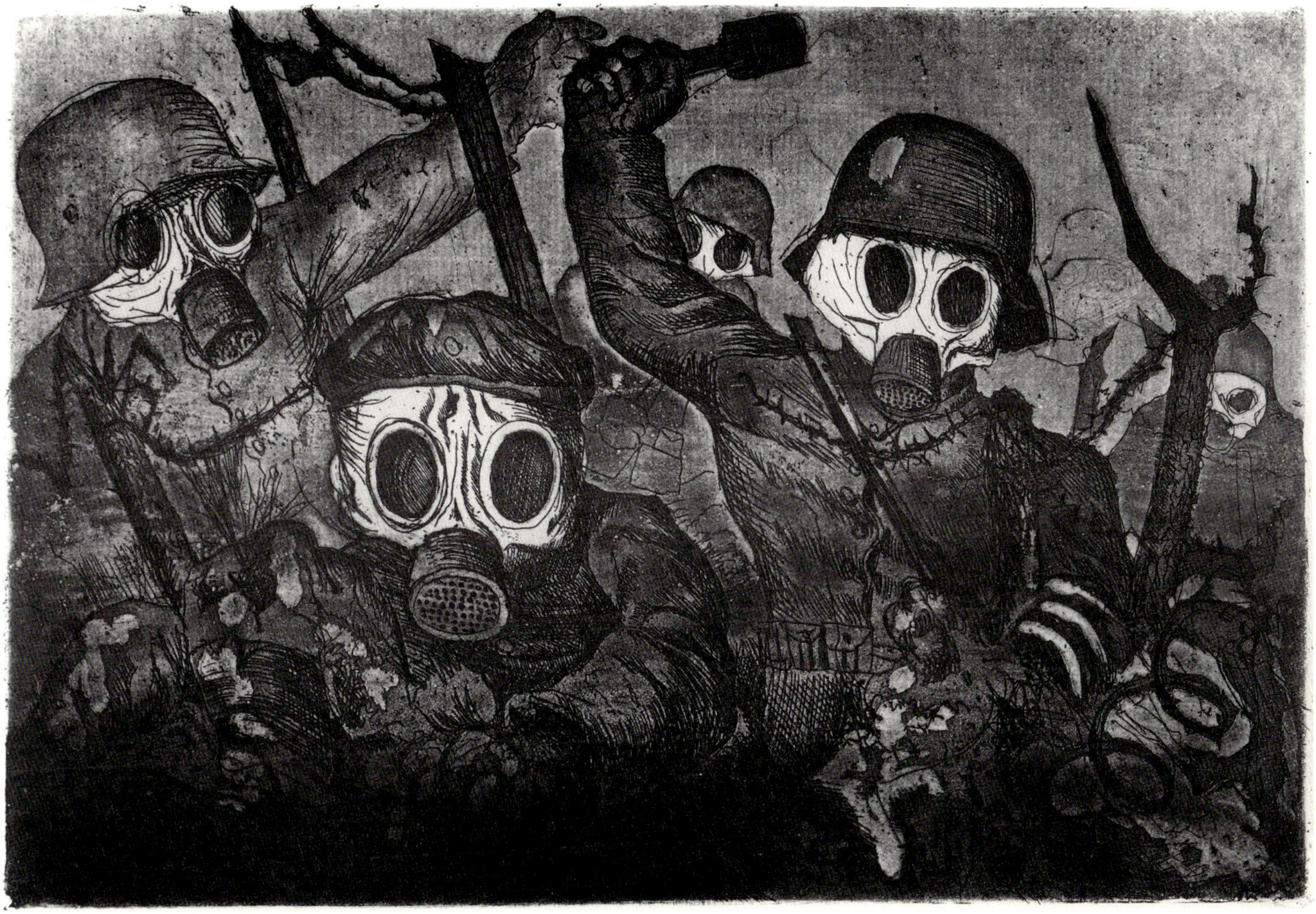

Plate 12
Stormtroops advance under gas

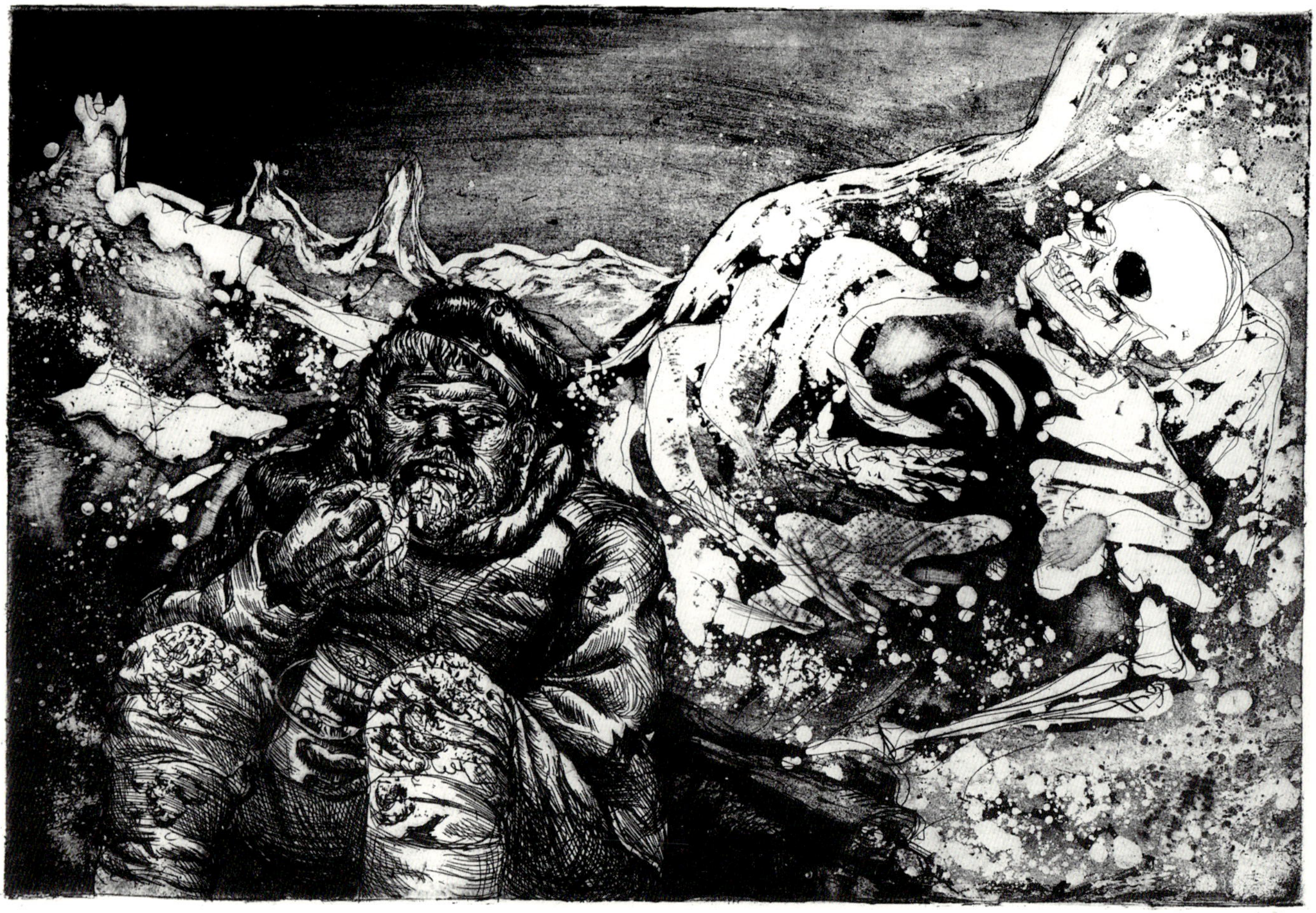

Plate 13
Meal-time in the ditch (Loretto heights)

On 30 January 1933 Hitler, most famous of the world's failed artists, became Chancellor; on 27 February the Reichstag Fire allowed him to start eliminating all opposition; on 21 March the Weimar Republic was liquidated to make room for the Third Reich. On 8 April Manfred von Killinger, the Reich Commissar for Saxony, had Dix ('that swine') removed from the Dresden Academy, which was now headed by Grosz's old bête noire Richard Müller, a new recruit to the Nazi Party. Then in mid-May Dix was asked to resign from the Prussian Academy, along with all the other left-wing appointees to that eminent body; he got no pension. In the course of that summer most of the museum and gallery directors favourable to modern art were removed, naturally including Paul Ferdinand Schmidt from Dresden. Of the artists there Griebel and Hans Gründig finished up in Sachsenhausen concentration camp; Erich Ohser was eventually executed; others, like Günther, were forbidden to paint; Dix was briefly arrested in 1939.

Even before the end of 1933 Müller organised 'purges of filth and muck' from the city collections, culminating in a show of 'illustrations of the decline of German art' in the town hall. Fortunately Dix was a friend of Fritz Lenk, one of the advisers to Goebbels's powerful Art Chamber - the new monolithic art organisation - and this enabled him to become a member. In 1934 he prudently moved to the south-east corner of Germany, where he built a house, not far from those of Erich Heckel, Walther Kaesbach and the photographer Hugo Erfurth. Turning to landscape painting, which he had effectively abandoned before the First War, he pursued the tradition favoured by the Nazis - a mélange of Albrecht Altdorfer, the Brueghels, Hans Baldung Grien. Such pictures he was able to sell, and even to exhibit with Nierendorf in Berlin.

The real attack on Dix came as part of the purge of the German public collections under the leadership of the Munich painter of nudes Adolf Ziegler, the Art Chamber's tasteful president, and it centred on his notorious undermining of the military spirit and his 'degradation of the German front-line soldier'. Ziegler had been commissioned by Hitler on 30 June 1937 to select 'works of decadent art in the sphere of painting and sculpture since 1910', initially for showing in that year's Degenerate Art Exhibition, and subsequently for sale abroad or ultimate burning. One of this man's aides was the painter Wolf Willrich, a former prisoner of war and student at the Dresden Academy from 1920-27, whose ensuing book on *Cleansing the Temple of Art* 'in the spirit of the Nordic Race' commented thus on the final plate of *Der Krieg*:

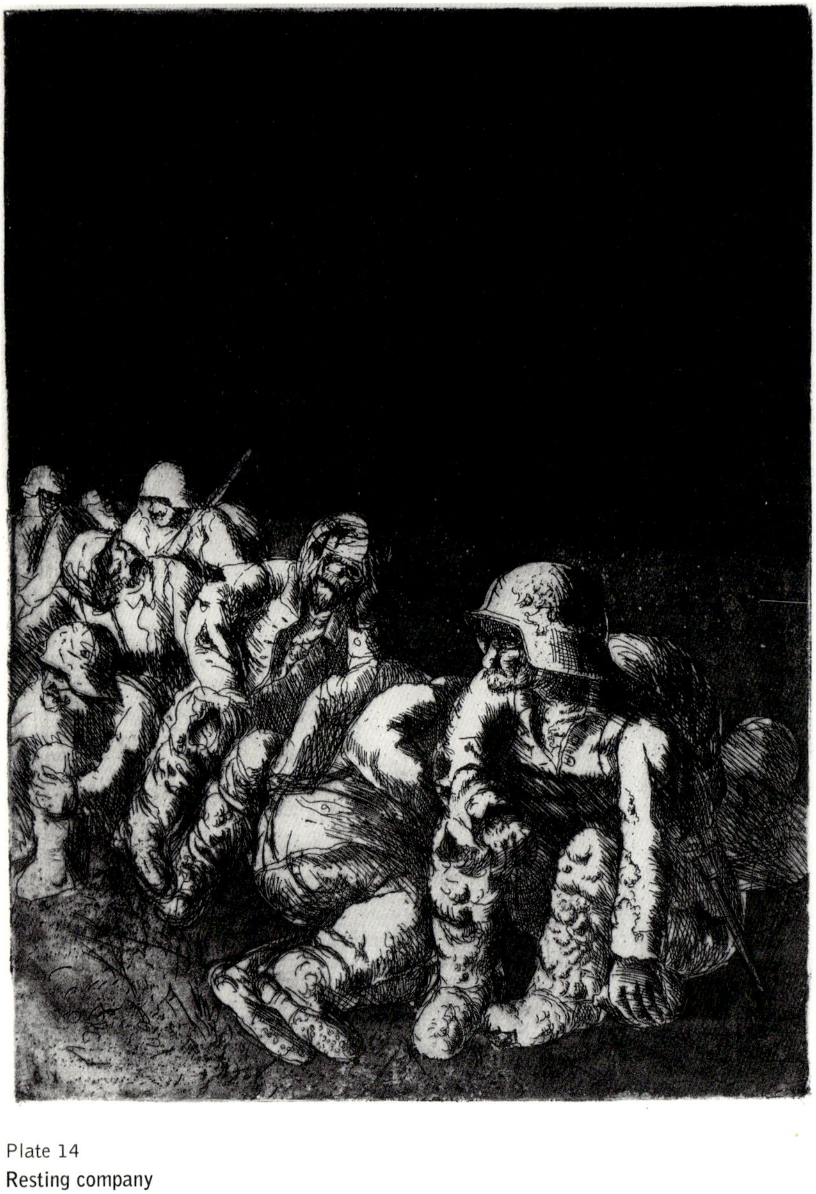

Plate 14
Resting company

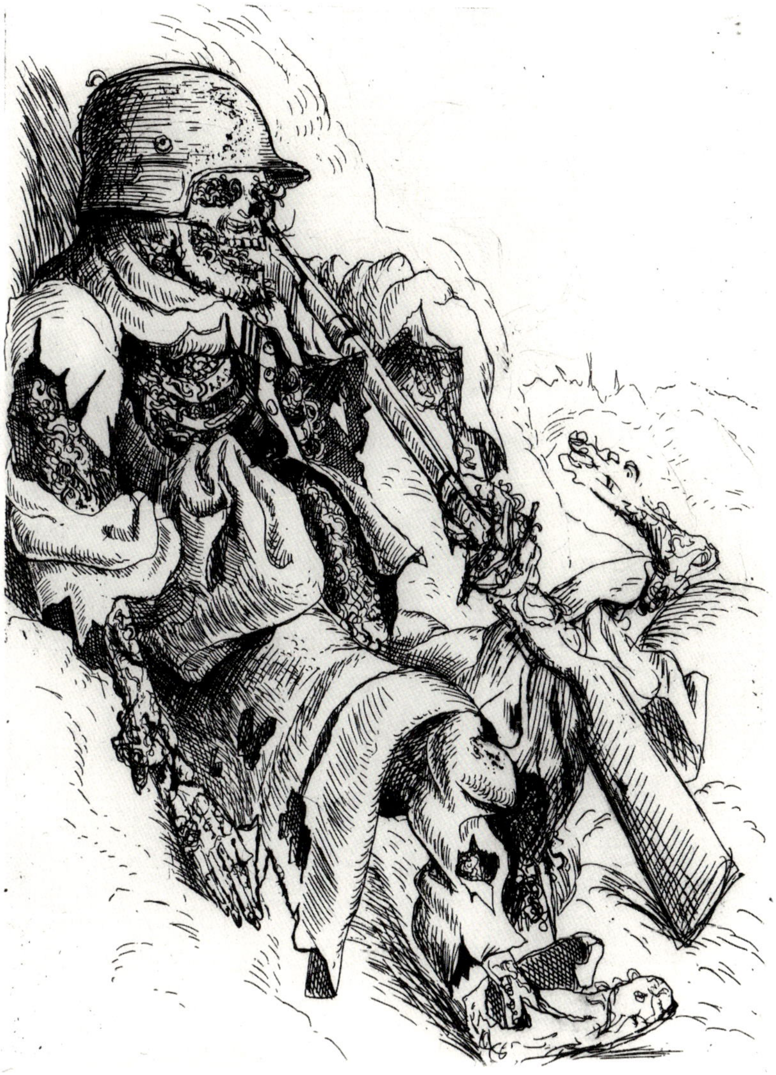

Plate 18
Dead sentry in a trench

> Here is a notably competent draughtsman making subtle use of all the various possibilities provided by drypoint and etching techniques for the conduct of a bolshevistic anti-war campaign . . .

The catalogue of that exhibition included nine of Dix's paintings, of which the Dada *War Cripples* and *The Trench* were in the big Room 3 and two working-class pictures of the same period in Room G2 downstairs, along with the Berlin Kupferstichkabinett's complete set of *Der Krieg* in Room G1. In all, 260 of Dix's works were purged, as against 151 by Felixmüller and 285 by George Grosz.

o

Looking at *Der Krieg* more than a century after the artist's birth, one has little sense of any propagandist 'campaign'; nor is there evidence of shrewd mockery as found in nearly all the German work by Grosz; the individualised faces of the ordinary soldiers are neither critically nor distortedly portrayed. If there are hints of the artist's own features they seem to recall his participation. He too was there; like Goya he is saying 'I saw it'. This is a feeling that is not present in any other comparable wartime cycle since Jacques Callot. Frans Masereel's passionate ink drawings and woodcuts are mostly those of a deeply concerned outsider, painfully observing from the margin. The Franco-Swiss Félix Vallotton's woodcuts *C'est la Guerre!* show the battlefield, but in a style that carries on from his anarchist prints in the old *Revue Blanche*. Henry Tonks's little-known watercolours of shattered faces are appalling but objective, like Dix's plate 40 and the photographs in Ernst Friedrich's *War Against War*; they were not made for publication. There are traces of a similar approach to Dix's in Ludwig Meidner's apocalyptic drawings from the eve of that war, and in the occasional plate by Beckmann; Pechstein's etchings of the Somme are also impressive, but they have nothing like the same richness and variety. The one truly comparable series, by its timing (from 1922 on), its scale (58 plates, plus some 40 rejects), its use of etching and aquatint, and its over-arching grandeur, is the *Miserere et Guerre* of Georges Rouault, though its feeling is notably more reflective and religious and it was not published until after the next great war.

In the East German re-edition of *Der Krieg* there is a quotation from a letter home written by an unidentified soldier in 1943, the year of the Battle of Stalingrad and the surrender in North Africa:

> I often find myself having to think of some pictures I saw long ago in an illustrated paper. Probably because they were accompanied by an article ridiculing them, I felt repelled and couldn't understand them. I've forgotten the artist's name. But his pictures won't let me alone. One of a wounded soldier, gazing into emptiness like a madman; another of a ghastly mining landscape. A stretch of ripped-up earth like where we lie at the moment. You will know what I'm trying to say. For the first time I understand the indictment which those pictures contain.

The force which was in them twenty years earlier was still there. Has anything happened since then to make it irrelevant today?

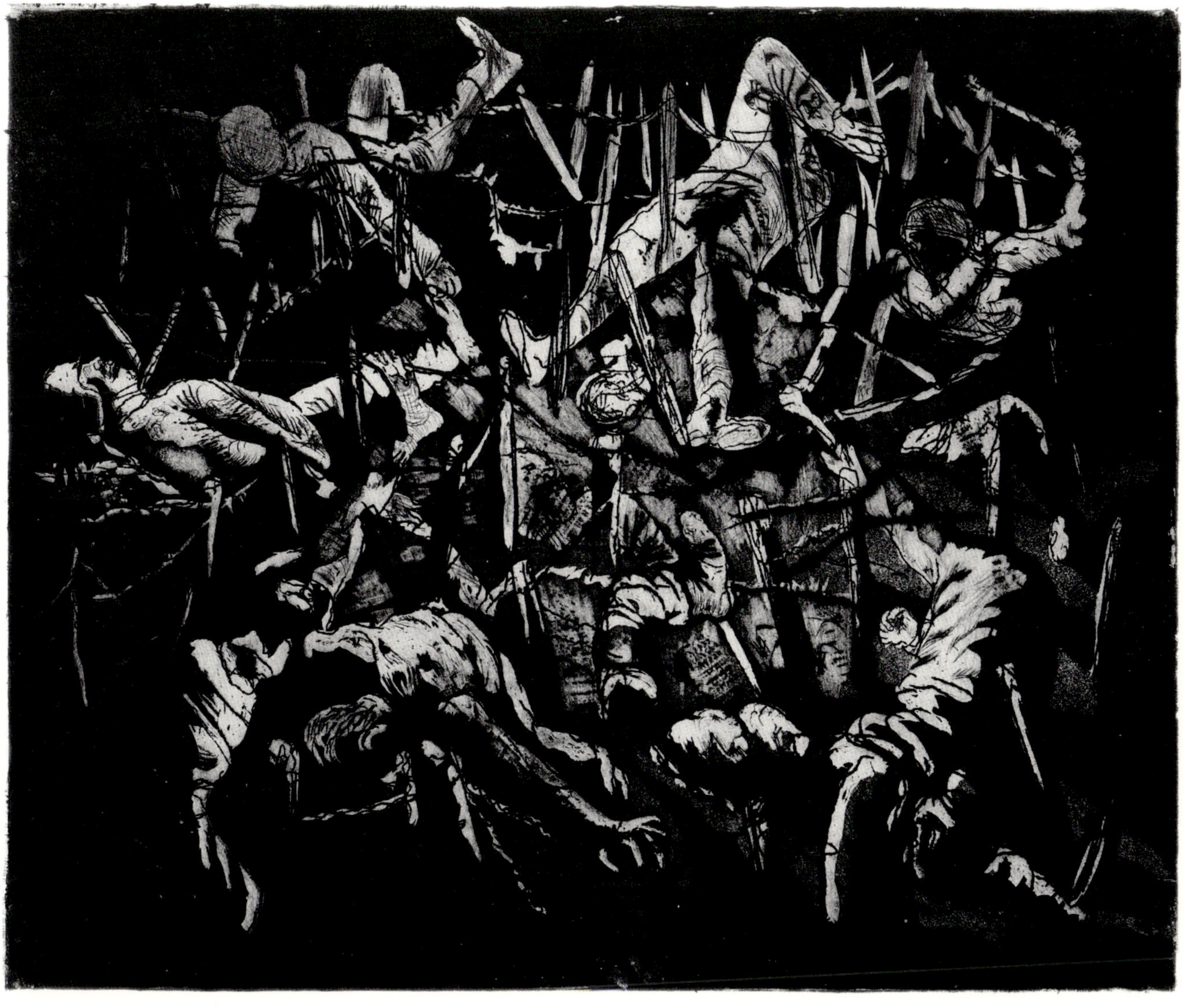

Plate 19
Dance of death, 1917 (the dead man's mound)

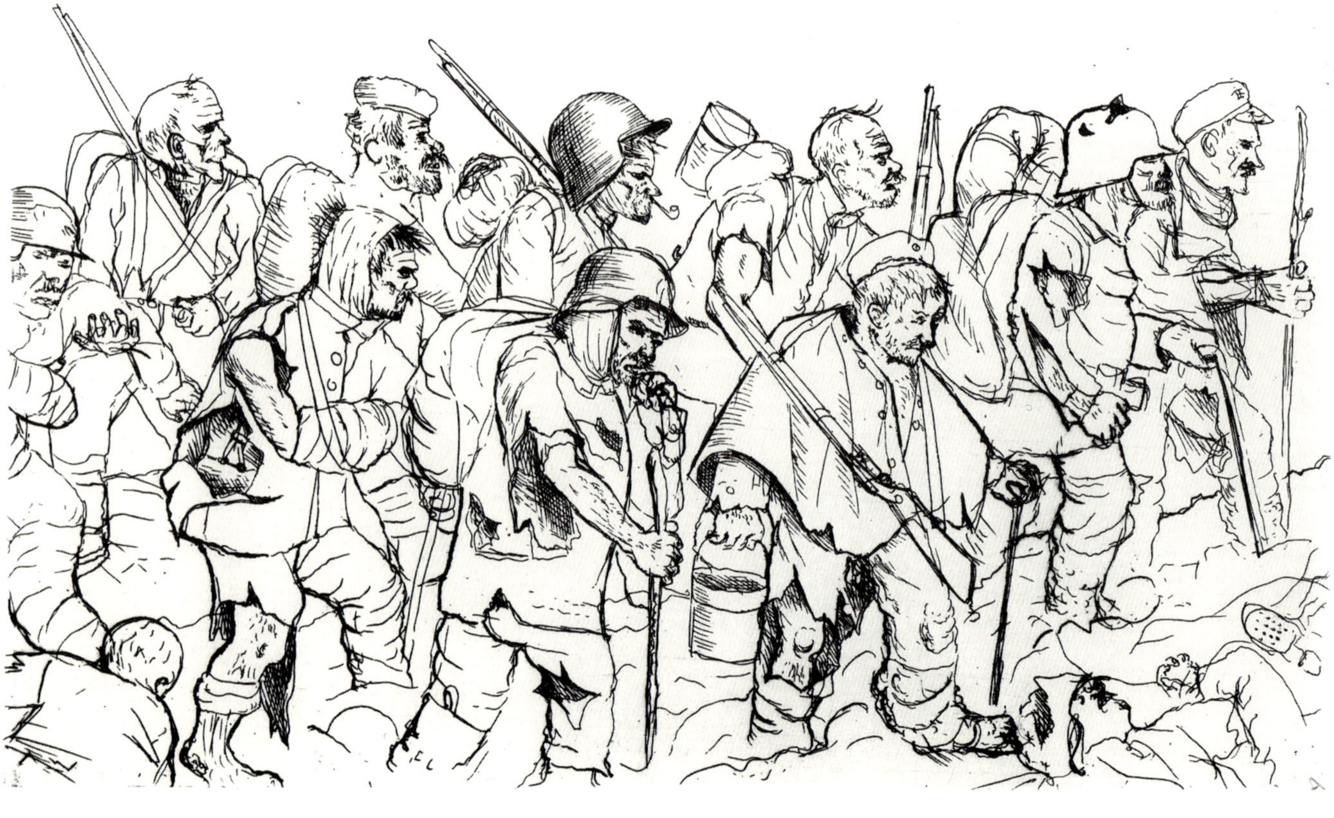

Plate 21

Exhausted troops retreat (Battle of the Somme)

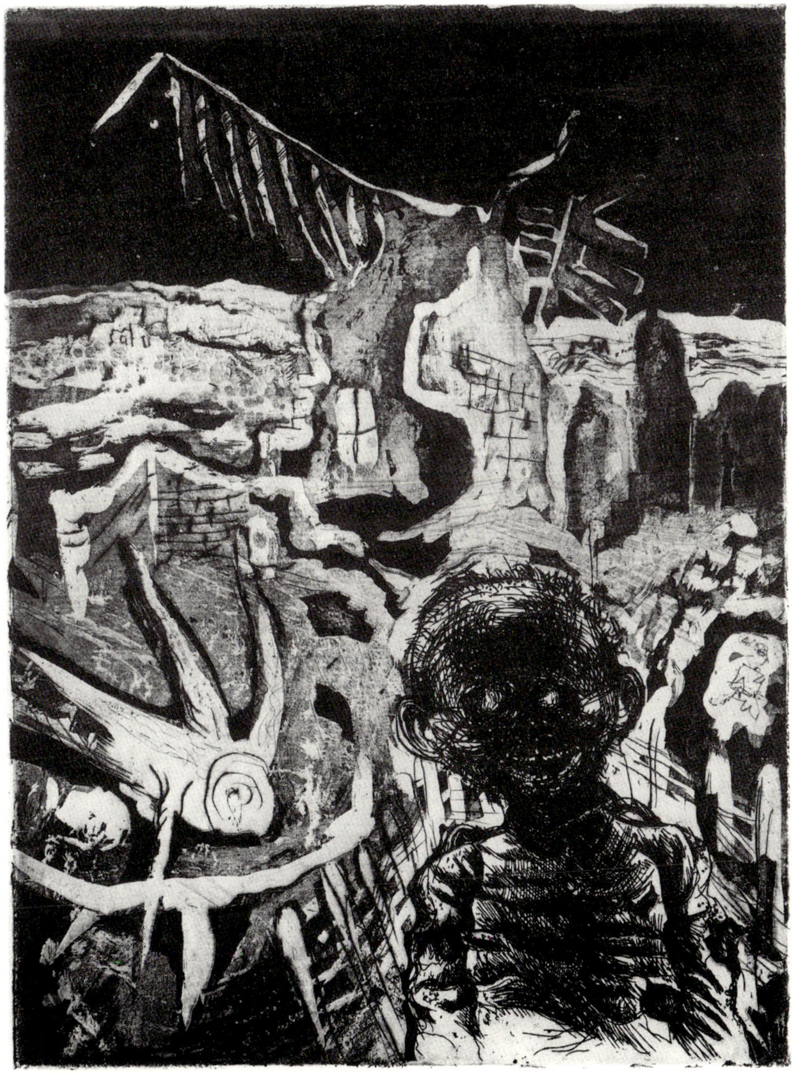

Plate 22
Nocturnal meeting with a madman

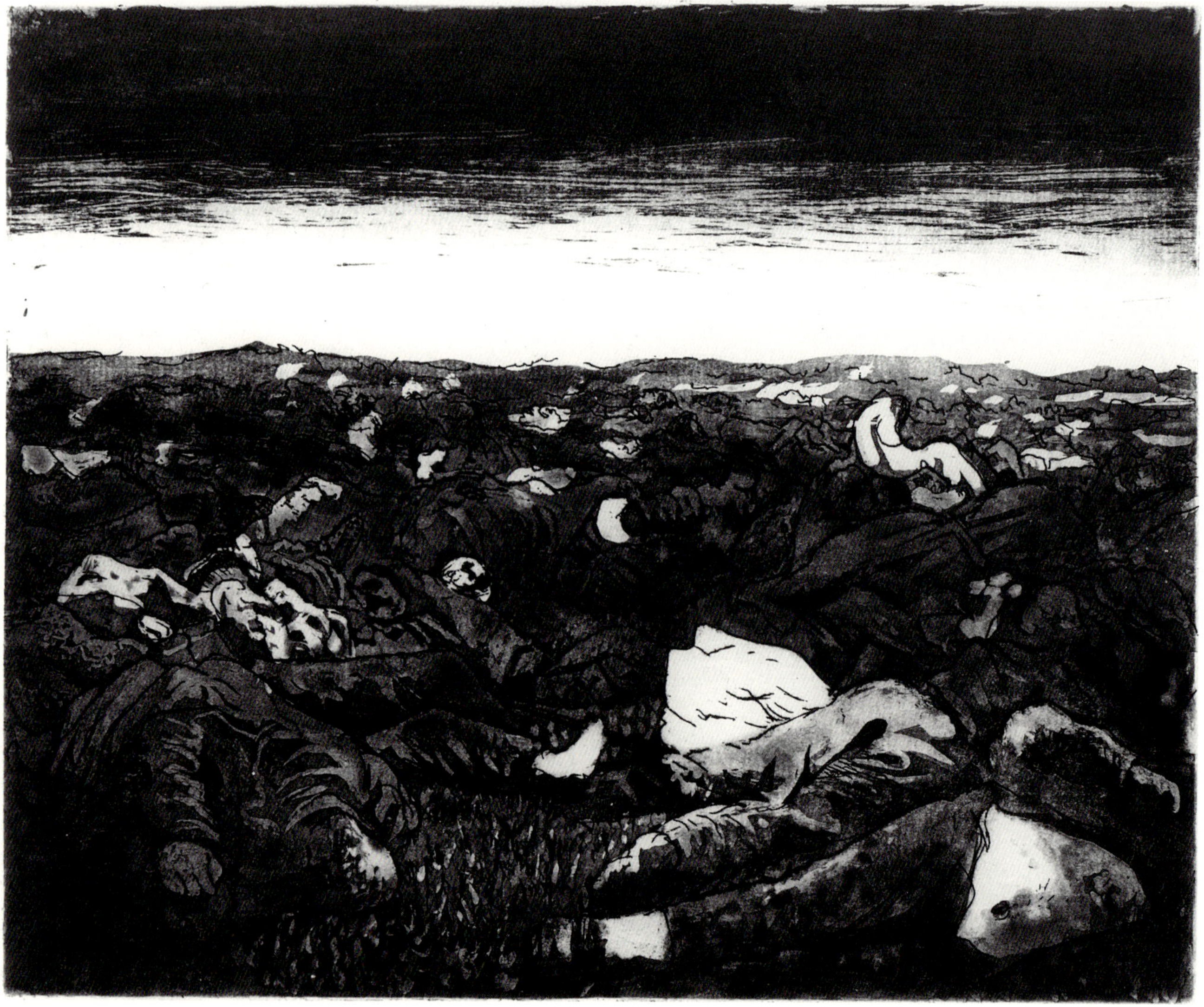

Plate 27
Evening in the Wijtschaete plain (Nov 1917)

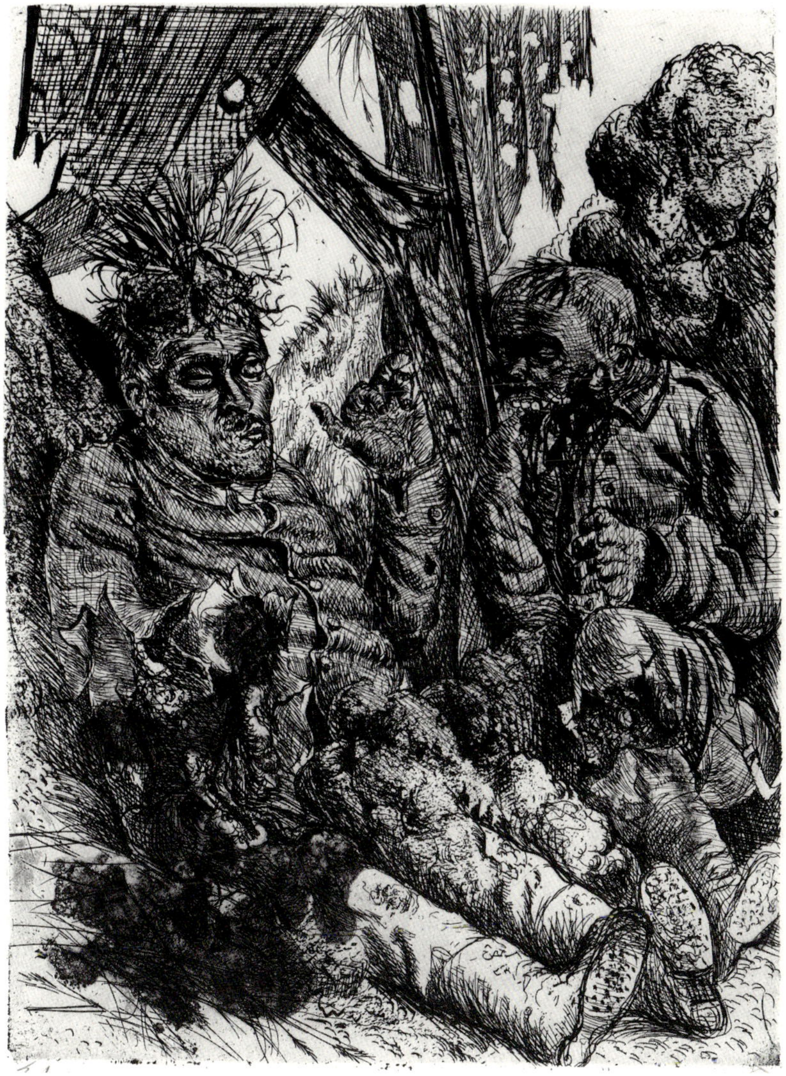

Plate 28
Seen at the steep slope at Cléry-sur-Somme

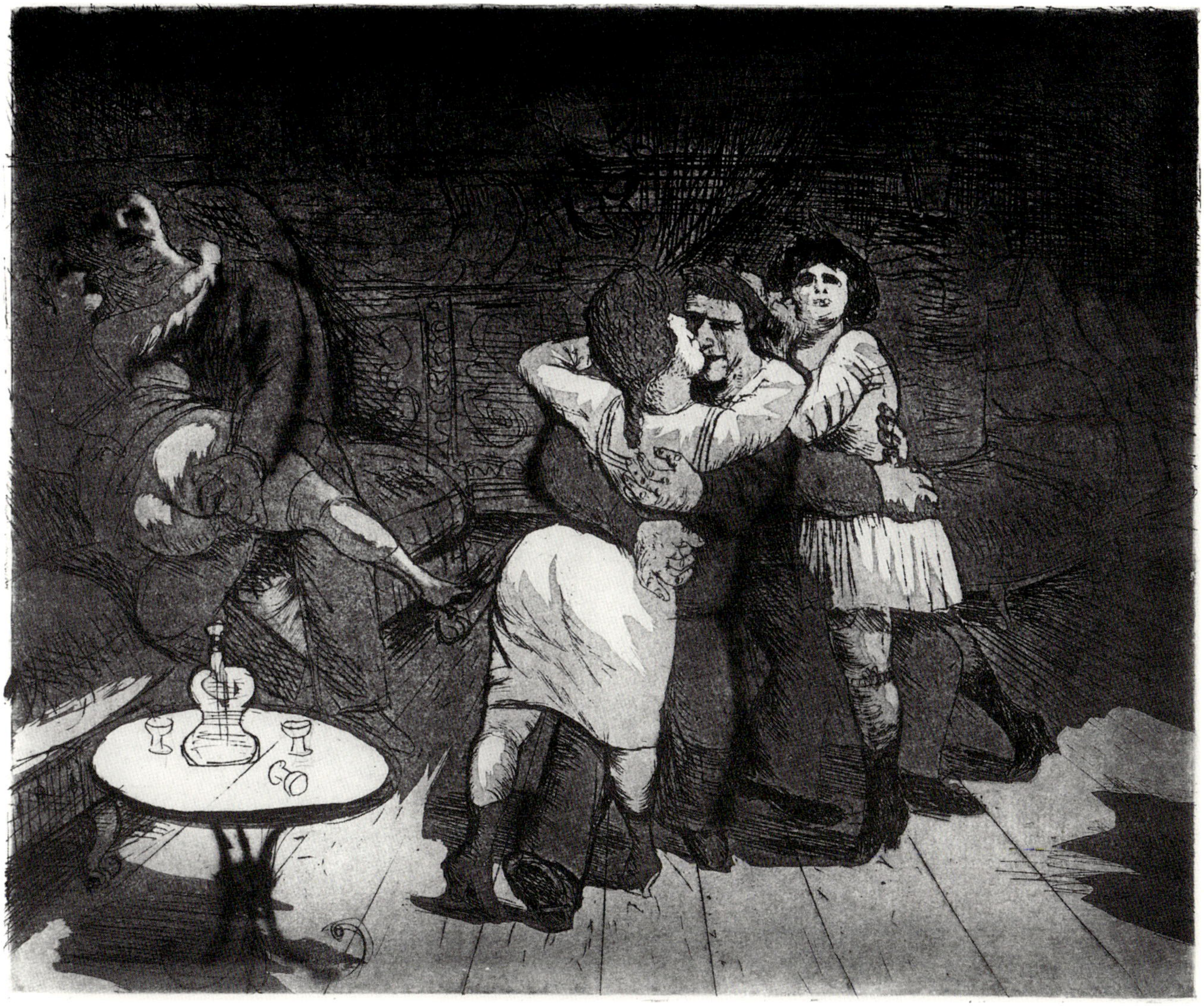

Plate 32
Sailors in Antwerp

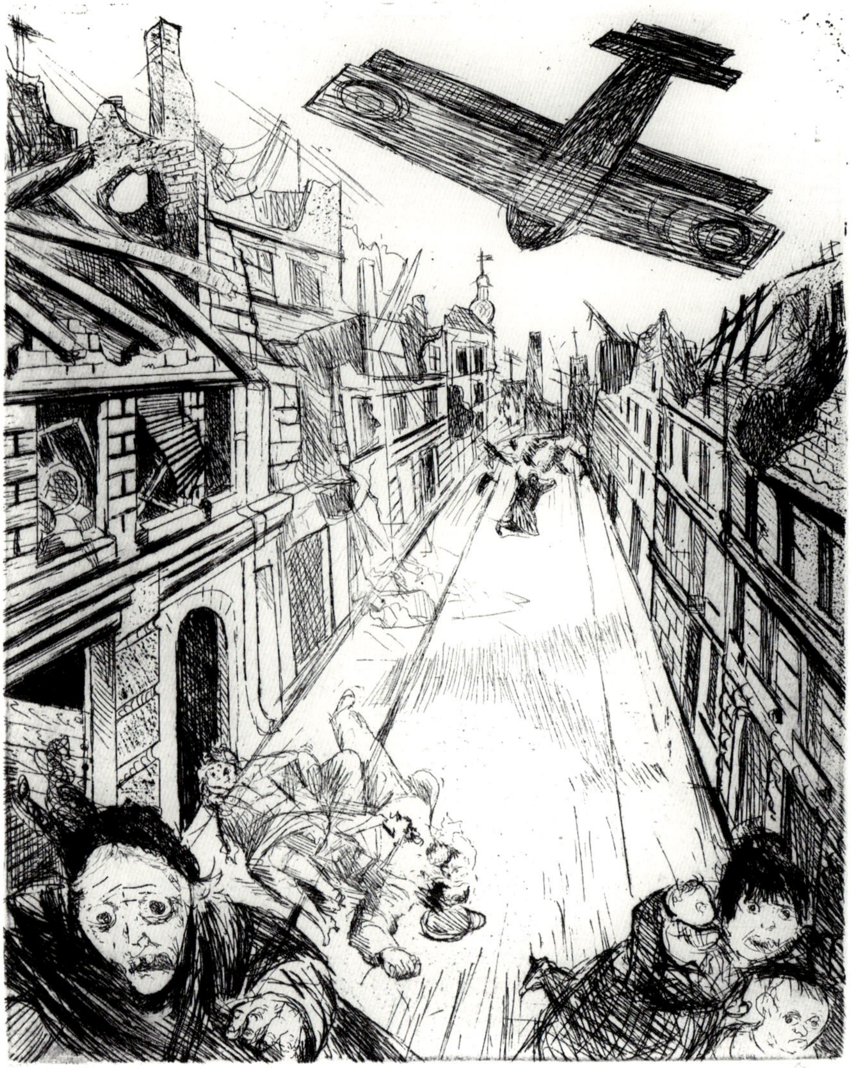

Plate 33
Lens is attacked with bombs

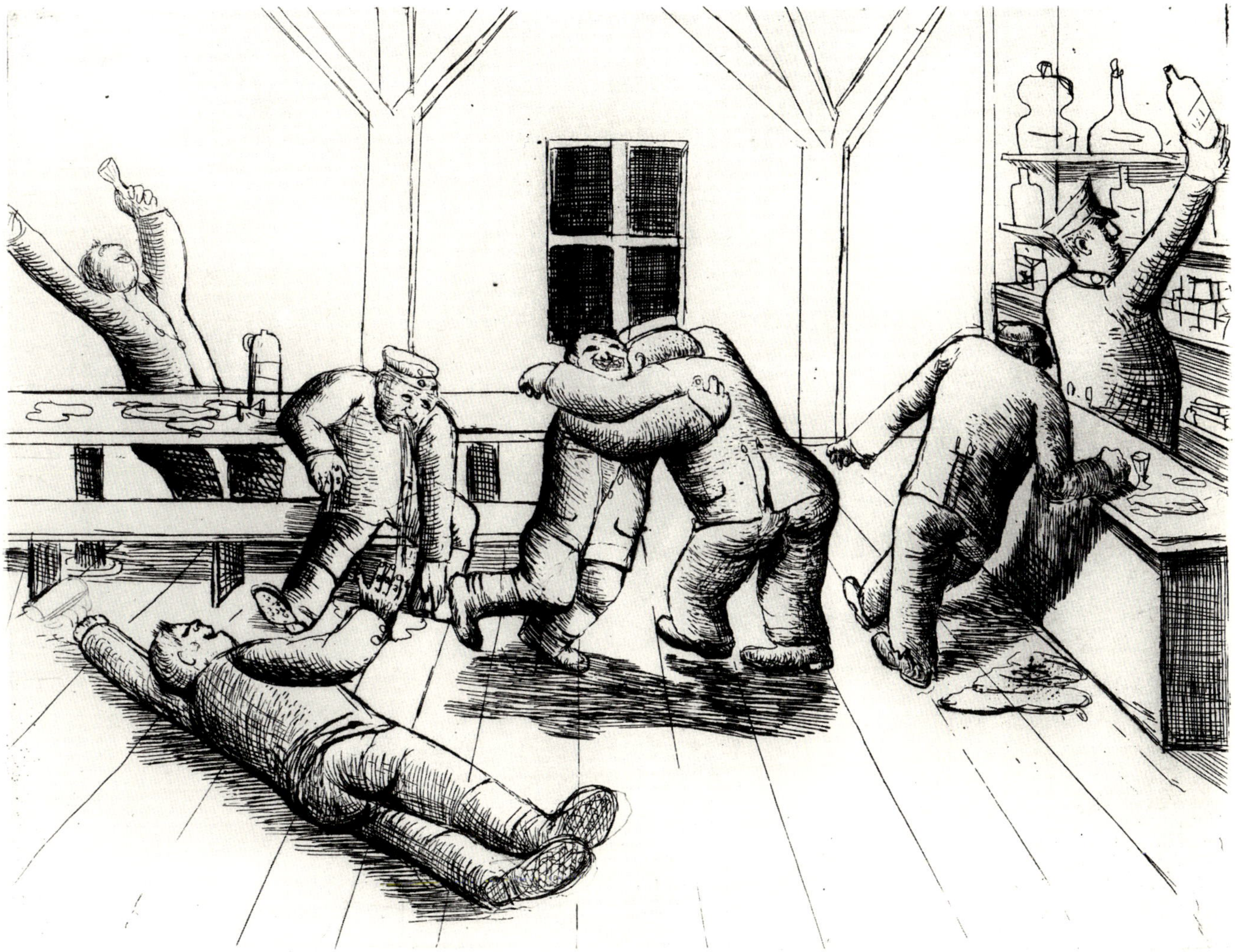

Plate 37
Mess in Haplincourt

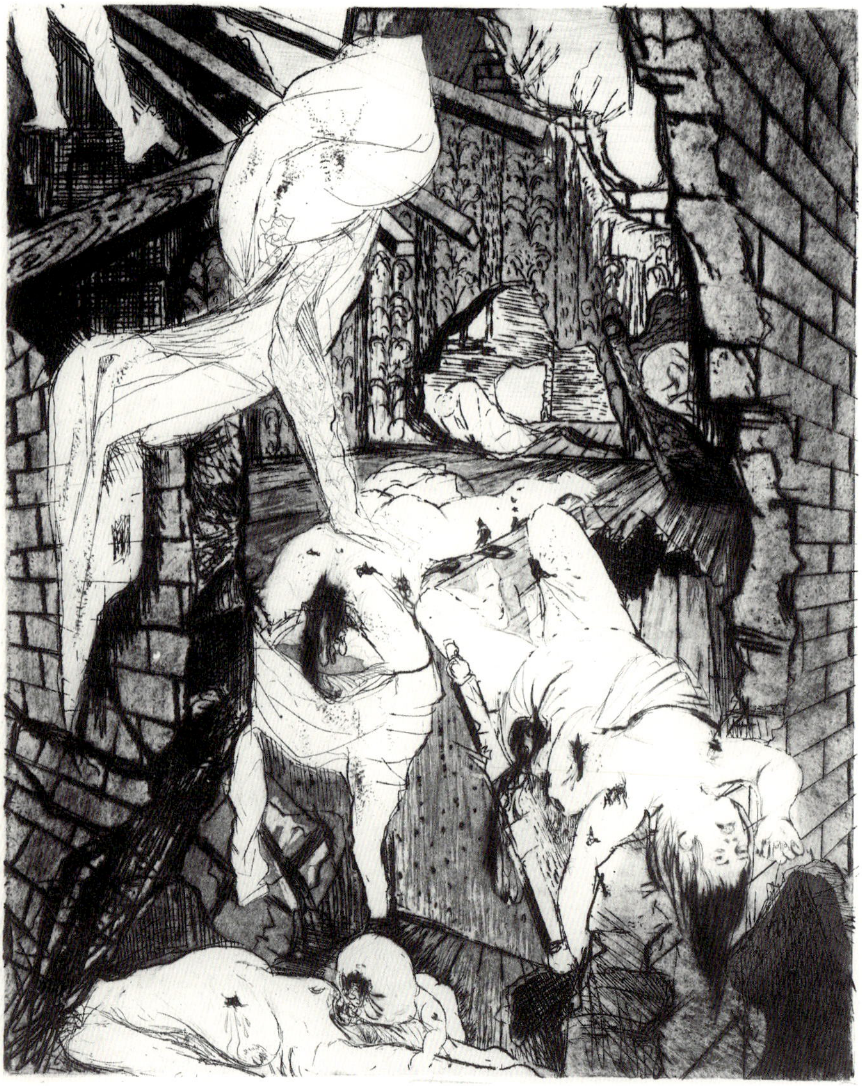

Plate 39

House destroyed by bombs (Tournai)

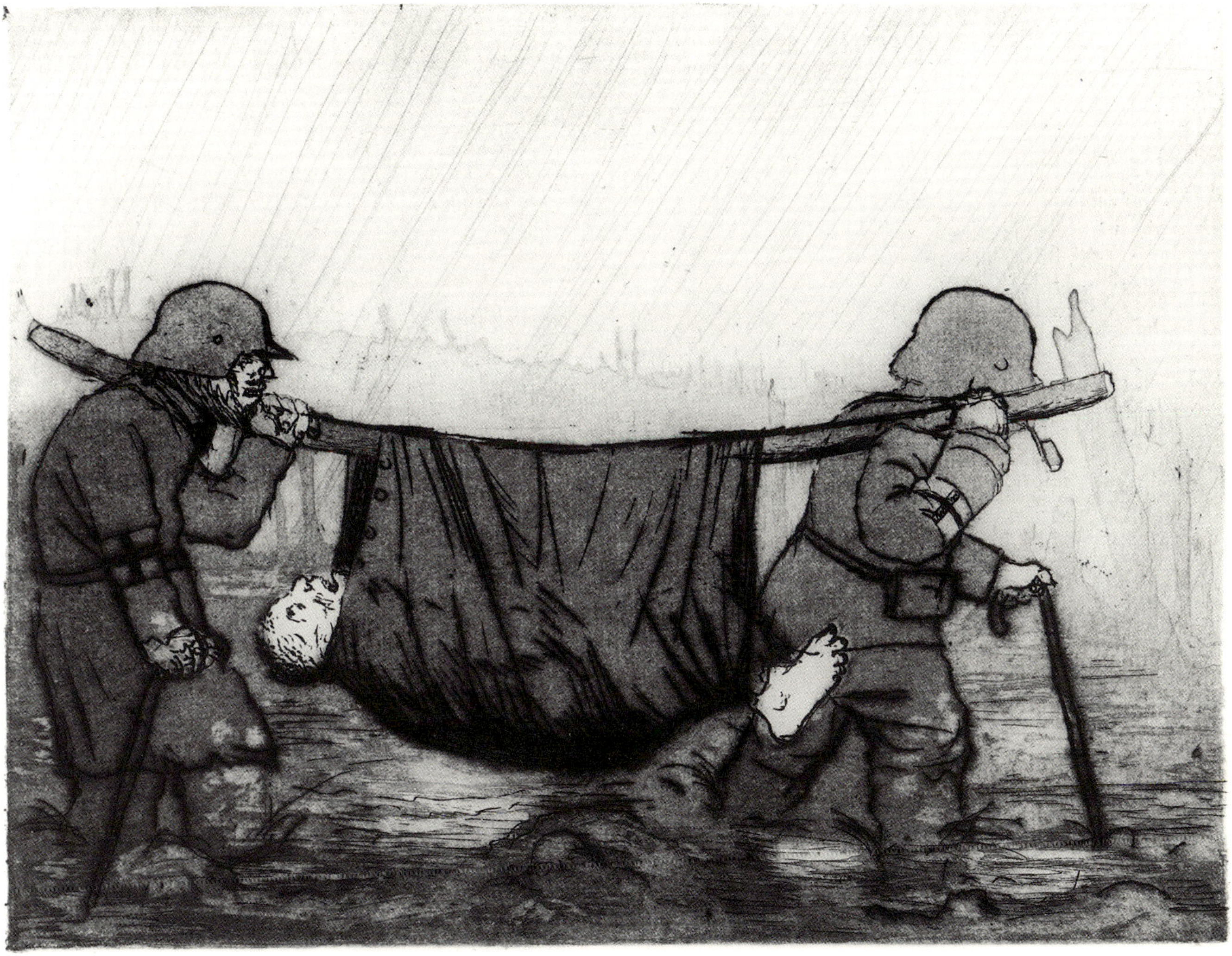

Plate 47

Carrying the wounded in Houthulster Wood

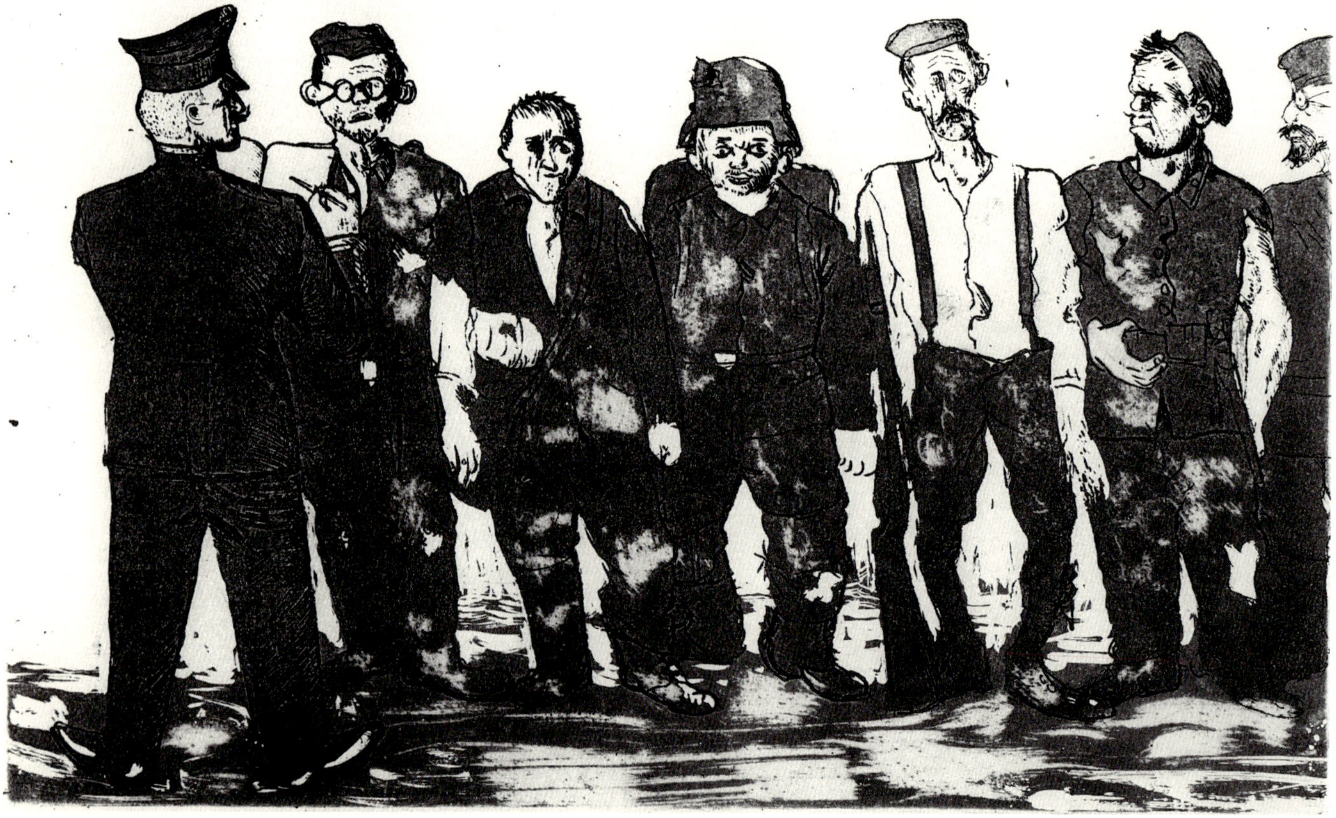

Plate 49
Roll-call of the returned

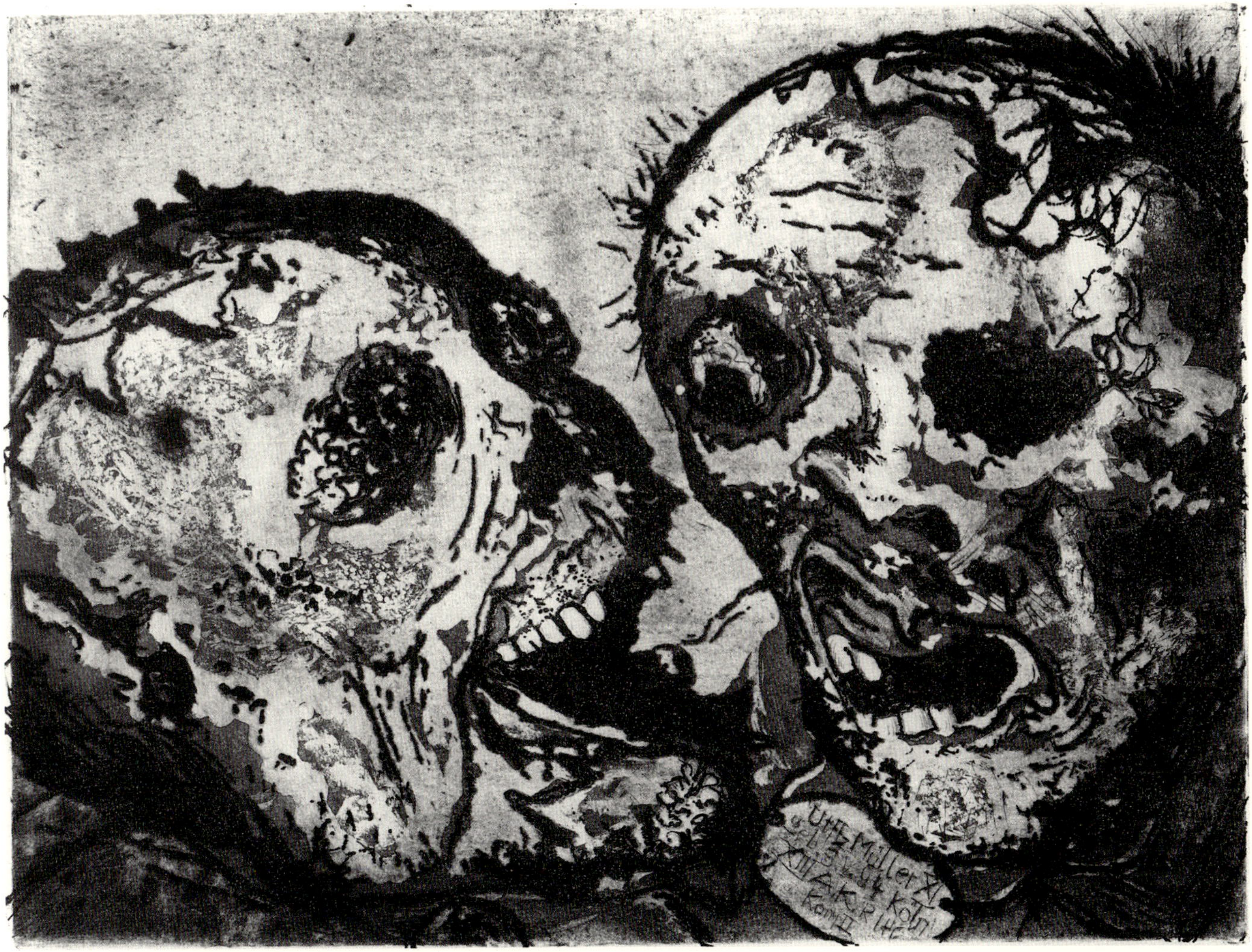

Plate 50
Dead men before the position at Tahure

Lists of Works

This exhibition contains a selection from each of the series.
All works are from the British Museum's Department of Prints and Drawings.
The registration numbers are those of the British Museum.

Measurements are in centimetres, height x width.

Asterisks indicate those plates which are illustrated in this catalogue.

Jacques Callot

Miseries of War, 1633
(large format)

Plate 1
Title plate
etching
8.9 x 19 cm
1861-7-13-757

Plate 2
Recruitment of troops
etching
7.6 x 18.5 cm
1861-7-13-760

Plate 3 *
Battle scene
etching
7.4 x 18.5 cm
1861-7-13-763

Plate 4
Scene of pillage
etching
7.5 x 18.6 cm
1861-7-13-766

Plate 5
Plundering a large farmhouse
etching
7.3 x 18.5 cm
1861-7-13-769

Plate 6
Destruction of a convent
etching
7.3 x 18.5 cm
1861-7-13-772

Plate 7
Plundering and burning a village
etching
7.4 x 18.5 cm
1861-7-13-775

Plate 8
Attack on a coach
etching
7.5 x 18.5 cm
1861-7-13-778

Plate 9
Discovery of the criminals
etching
7.7 x 18.6 cm
1861-7-13-781

Plate 10 *
The strappado
etching
7.4 x 19 cm
1861-7-13-784

Plate 11 *
The hanging
etching
7.2 x 18.5 cm
1861-7-13-787

Plate 12 *
The firing squad
etching
7.3 x 18.5 cm
1861-7-13-789

Plate 13 *
The stake
etching
7.3 x 18.6 cm
1861-7-13-792

Plate 14 *
The wheel
etching
7.3 x 18.4 cm
1861-7-13-794

Plate 15
The hospital
etching
7.3 x 18.5 cm
1861-7-13-796

Plate 16
Dying men by the roadside
etching
7.5 x 18.5 cm
1861-7-13-799

Plate 17 *
The peasants avenge themselves
etching
7.5 x 18.6 cm
1861-7-13-802

Plate 18
Distribution of awards
etching
7.4 x 18.5 cm
1861-7-13-804

Miseries of War, 1636
(small format)

Title plate (not by Callot)
etching
5.5 x 11.5 cm
1861-7-13-750

Plate 1
Camp scene
etching
5.4 x 11.5 cm
1861-7-13-751

Plate 2 *
Attack on the highway
etching
5.5 x 11.5 cm
1861-7-13-752

Plate 3 *
Destruction of a convent
etching
5.1 x 11.5 cm
1861-7-13-753

Plate 4 *
Plundering and burning a village
etching
5.5 x 11.5 cm
1861-7-13-754

Plate 5
The peasants avenge themselves
etching
5.6 x 11.5 cm
1861-7-13-755

Plate 6
The hospital
etching
5.1 x 11.5 cm
1861-7-13-756

Francisco Goya y Lucientes

The Disasters of War, 1810-20
(this edition published in 1863)

Plate 1 *
Dire forebodings of what is going to happen
Tristes presentimientos de lo que ha de acontecer
etching, drypoint, burin and burnisher
17.8 x 22 cm
1975-10-25-196

Plate 2 *
Rightly or wrongly
Con razon ó sin ella
etching, lavis, drypoint, burin and burnisher
15 x 20.9 cm
1975-10-25-197

Plate 3
The same
Lo mismo
etching, lavis, drypoint, burin and burnisher
16.2 x 22.3 cm
1975-10-25-198

Plate 5 *
And they are like wild beasts
Y son fieras
etching, burnished aquatint and drypoint
15.8 x 21 cm
1975-10-25-201

Plate 7 *
What courage!
Que valor!
etching, aquatint, drypoint, burin and burnisher
15.8 x 20.9 cm
1975-10-25-203

Plate 9
They don't want to
No quieren
etching, aquatint, drypoint and burin
15.6 x 20.9 cm
1975-10-25-206

Plate 11
Nor do these
Ni por esas
etching, lavis, drypoint and burin
16.2 x 21.3 cm
1975-10-25-209

Plate 13
Bitter presence
Amarga presencia
etching, lavis, burin and burnisher
14.3 x 16.9 cm
1975-10-25-211

Plate 14 *
Hard is the way!
Duro es el paso!
etching, burnished lavis, drypoint and burin
14.3 x 16.8 cm
1975-10-25-212

Plate 15 *
And there's nothing one can do about it
Y no hai remedio
etching, drypoint, burin and burnisher
14.2 x 16.8 cm
1975-10-25-214

Plate 16 *
They help themselves
Se aprovechan
etching, lavis, drypoint, burin and burnisher
16.2 x 23.7 cm
1975-10-25-215

Plate 18 *
Bury them, without a word
Enterrar y callar
etching, burnished lavis, drypoint and burin
16.3 x 23.7 cm
1975-10-25-218

Plate 19 *
It's already too late
Ya no hay tiempo
etching, lavis, drypoint, burin and burnisher
16.6 x 23.9 cm
1975-10-25-220

Plate 22
Even worse
Tanto y mas
etching, lavis and burin
16.2 x 25.3 cm
1975-10-25-224

Plate 24
They could still come in useful
Aun podrán servir
etching and burnisher
16.3 x 26 cm
1975-10-25-227

Plate 26 *
One can't watch this
No se puede mirar
etching, lavis, drypoint and burin
14.5 x 21 cm
1975-10-25-230

Plate 27 *
Charity
Caridad
etching, lavis, drypoint, burin and burnisher
16.3 x 23.6 cm
1975-10-25-231

Plate 30 *
Ravages of war
Estragos de la guerra
etching, drypoint, burin and burnisher
14.1 x 17 cm
1975-10-25-236

Plate 32
Why?
Por qué
etching, lavis, burin and burnisher
15.7 x 20.9 cm
1975-10-25-239

Plate 33
What more could possibly be done?
Qué hai que hacer mas?
etching, lavis, burin and burnisher
15.7 x 20.7 cm
1975-10-25-241

Plate 35 *
One can't tell why
No se puede saber por qué
etching, burnished lavis, drypoint and burin
15.4 x 25.6 cm
1975-10-25-245

Plate 36
Nor in this case either
Tampoco
etching, burnished aquatint,
drypoint and burin
15.7 x 20.8 cm
1975-10-25-247

Plate 37
This is worse
Esto es peor
etching, lavis and drypoint
15.7 x 20.8 cm
1975-10-25-249

Plate 38 *
Barbarians!
Bárbaros!
etching, burnished aquatint
and drypoint
15.5 x 20.8 cm
1975-10-25-250

Plate 39 *
What a feat! With dead men!
Grande hazaña! Con muertos!
etching, lavis and drypoint
15.6 x 20.8 cm
1975-10-25-251

Plate 44 *
I saw this
Yo lo vi
etching, drypoint and burin
16.1 x 23.9 cm
1975-10-25-257

Plate 45
And this too
Y esto tambien
etching, lavis, aquatint, drypoint
and burin
16.6 x 22.2 cm
1975-10-25-258

Plate 48
Cruel tale of woe!
Cruel Lástima!
etching, burnished lavis and burin
15.1 x 20.8 cm
1975-10-25-263

Plate 50 *
Wretched mother!
Madre infeliz!
etching, burnished aquatint and
drypoint
15.7 x 20.6 cm
1975-10-25-266

Plate 51
Thanks to the millet
Gracias á la almorta
etching and burnished aquatint
15.6 x 20.7 cm
1975-10-25-267

Plate 55 *
The worst is to beg
Lo peor es pedir
etching, lavis and burnisher
15.6 x 20.8 cm
1975-10-25-271

Plate 63
A heap of dead bodies
Muertos recogidos
etching and burnished aquatint
15.5 x 20.8 cm
1975-10-25-280

Plate 69 *
Nothing. Time will tell
Nada. Ello dirá
etching, burnished aquatint,
lavis and drypoint
15.5 x 20.1 cm
1975-10-25-288

Otto Dix

Der Krieg, 1924 (War)

Plate 3 *
Men killed by gas (Templeux-La-Fosse, August 1916)
Gastote (Templeux-La-Fosse, August 1916)
etching
19.4 x 28.7 cm
1982-7-24-28 (3)

Plate 4 *
Field of shell craters near Dontrien lit up by flares
Trichterfeld bei Dontrien, von Leuchtkugeln erhellt
etching printed in relief
19.3 x 25.4 cm
1982-7-24-28 (4)

Plate 5
Dead horse
Pferdekadaver
etching
14.2 x 19.3 cm
1982-7-24-28 (5)

Plate 6 *
Wounded (Autumn 1916, Bapaume)
Verwundeter (Herbst 1916, Bapaume)
etching and aquatint
19.3 x 28.9 cm
1982-7-24-28 (6)

Plate 7 *
Near Langemark
Bei Langemark
etching
24.7 x 29.3 cm
1982-7-24-28 (7)

Plate 9 *
Destroyed trenches
Zerfallener Kampfgraben
etching, aquatint and roulette
29.8 x 24.4 cm
1982-7-24-28 (9)

Plate 10 *
Fleeing wounded man (Battle of the Somme 1916)
Fliehender Verwundeter (Sommeschlacht 1916)
etching
19.1 x 13.6 cm
1982-7-24-28 (10)

Plate 12 *
Stormtroops advance under gas
Sturmtruppe geht unter Gas vor
etching and aquatint
19.3 x 28.8 cm
1982-7-24-28 (12)

Plate 13 *
Meal-time in the ditch (Loretto heights)
Mahlzeit in der Sappe (Lorettohöhe)
etching and aquatint
19.1 x 28.8 cm
1982-7-24-28 (13)

Plate 14 *
Resting company
Ruhende Kompanie
etching and aquatint
25.5 x 19 cm
1982-7-24-28 (14)

Plate 18 *
Dead sentry in a trench
Toter Sappenposten
etching
19.1 x 14.2 cm
1982-7-24-28 (18)

Plate 19 *
Dance of death, 1917 (the dead man's mound)
Totentanz anno 17 (Höhe Toter Mann)
etching and aquatint
24.4 x 29.9 cm
1982-7-24-28 (19)

Plate 21 *
Exhausted troops retreat (Battle of the Somme)
Abgekämpfte Truppe geht zurück (Sommeschlacht)
etching
19.6 x 28.7 cm
1982-7-24-28 (21)

Plate 22 *
Nocturnal meeting with a madman
Nächtliche Begegnung mit einem Irrsinnigen
etching and aquatint
25.8 x 19.4 cm
1982-7-24-28 (22)

Plate 23
Dead man in mud
Toter im Schlamm
etching and aquatint
18.9 x 25.3 cm
1982-7-24-28 (23)

Plate 27 *
Evening in the Wijtschaete plain (Nov 1917)
Abends in der Wijtschaete-Ebene (Nov 1917)
etching and aquatint
23.9 x 29.5 cm
1982-7-24-28 (27)

Plate 28 *
Seen at the steep slope at Cléry-sur-Somme
Gesehen am Steilhang von Cléry-sur-Somme
etching and aquatint
25.7 x 19 cm
1982-7-24-28 (28)

Plate 32 *
Sailors in Antwerp
Matrosen in Antwerpen
etching and aquatint
23.8 x 29.5 cm
1982-7-24-28 (32)

Plate 33 *
Lens is attacked with bombs
Lens wird mit Bomben belegt
etching
29.7 x 24.4 cm
1982-7-24-28 (33)

Plate 36
Visit to Madame Germaine at Méricourt
Besuch bei Madame Germaine in Méricourt
etching and aquatint
25.7 x 19.3 cm
1982-7-24-28 (36)

Plate 37 *
Mess in Haplincourt
Kantine in Haplincourt
etching
19.2 x 25.7 cm
1982-7-24-28 (37)

Plate 39 *
House destroyed by bombs (Tournai)
Durch Fliegerbomben zerstörtes Haus (Tournai)
etching, engraving and aquatint
29.7 x 24.4 cm
1982-7-24-28 (39)

Plate 40
Transplant
Transplantation
etching and aquatint
19.4 x 14.3 cm
1982-7-24-28 (40)

Plate 41
Machine-gun party advances (Somme, November 1916)
Maschinengewehrzug geht vor (Somme, Nov. 1916)
etching and aquatint
24.3 x 29.8 cm
1982-7-24-28 (41)

Plate 47 *
Carrying the wounded in Houthulster Wood
Verwundetentransport im Houthulster Wald
etching and aquatint
19.5 x 25.7 cm
1982-7-24-28 (47)

Plate 49 *
Roll-call of the returned
Appell der Zurückgekehrten
etching and aquatint
19.6 x 28.6 cm
1982-7-24-28 (49)

Plate 50 *
Dead men before the position at Tahure
Tote vor der Stellung bei Tahure
etching and aquatint
19.4 x 25.8 cm
1982-7-24-28 (50)